Praise for *Talking in t*

Many people could write books on prayer, but not many could write a book like this. Steve Harper has lived the questions of life, experienced the mystery, and is honest enough to share his journey with us.

If you have been or are haunted by the question "Why pray?" this book is for you. If you are a bit beyond that question, you probably still need the book because someone you know is asking the question.

Though focused on prayer, *Talking in the Dark* will help readers with their questions and wonderings about how God relates to the whole of our lives. For me the book represents teaching and witness at their best—honest experience and practical guidance.

—MAXIE DUNNAM
Chancellor, Asbury Theological Seminary

God gifted Steve Harper with the ability to cut through theological jargon, clear a pathway to Jesus, and guide others into the embrace of the Comforter. Harper is absolutely right: Life does not always make sense, and he has the courage to speak with honesty about how that feels. *Talking in the Dark* invites us into painful spaces, agonizing questions, and hushed moments in order to be found by the great Companion of our lives.

—PAUL W. CHILCOTE, PHD
Visiting Professor of the Practice of Evangelism
Duke Divinity School

Read this book, and you'll probably feel as I did, that you are sitting with a friend who is willing to talk honestly about the struggles we have with prayer when life makes no sense. When you rise from this "conversation," likely you will feel that you have found more than an understanding friend—you have found a wise friend, one who provided the perspective you needed. Harper's book does not attempt to placate with simplistic answers but resonates with profound wisdom. The book is real and rings with truth because the author is honest, vulnerable, a man of faith, and insight. I can attest to this because he has been my friend for decades. After reading *Talking in the Dark*, you'll find him to be the kind of soul friend you have needed as well.

—C. REGINALD JOHNSON, PHD
Dean, School of Theology and Formation
Asbury Theological Seminary

TALKING IN THE DARK

PRAYING WHEN LIFE DOESN'T MAKE SENSE

STEVE HARPER

Talking in the Dark: Praying When Life Doesn't Make Sense

The Upper Room Web site: www.upperroom.org

At the time of publication all Web sites referenced in this book were valid. However, due to the fluid nature of the Internet, some addresses may have changed or the content may no longer be relevant.

Cover design: The DesignWorks Group / www.thedesignworksgroup.com
Cover image: iStockphoto
Interior design: Nter Design / www.nterdesign.com
First printing: 2007

Library of Congress Cataloging-in-Publication Data

Harper, Steve.
Talking in the dark : praying when life doesn't make sense / Steve Harper.
p. cm.
ISBN 978-0-8358-9922-2
1. Prayer—Christianity. I. Title.
BV210.3.H365 2007
248.3'2—dc22

2007000451

Printed in the United States of America

For Jeannie
My conversation partner in the dark

CONTENTS

INTRODUCTION

Life doesn't make sense. No matter how hard we try to make it so, it doesn't. No matter how much we want everything to turn out okay, it doesn't always. Bad things happen to good people, and good things happen to bad people. That's the way it is. If we are religious, prayer gets mixed into the mystery and the frustration of that reality. Sometimes we can't tell what difference prayer is making. Even though we pray, life falls short of our sense of justice and cry for mercy.

What you are about to read was conceived nearly twenty years ago. I was conducting a prayer workshop at a church. In the midst of a session, a man raised his hand. When I called on him, he said words to this effect: "I appreciate what you're saying, and I believe most of it. But you aren't dealing with the question that motivated me to attend this workshop. I really want to know only one thing: Can you tell me why I should keep praying?" He did not go into detail, but clearly life had dealt him blows that made it difficult to continue praying. His question put a hush over the session. I did not have a satisfactory answer for him, I'm sure. He stayed for the rest of the workshop, but every time I looked his way, his question reverberated in my soul. It has continued to do so, because in reality it is my question as well.

Sometimes I think God has called me to speak, write, and teach about prayer so I will not give up on it altogether. After more than forty years of praying, I still do not understand prayer. I still do not practice it as I would like. I have as many—perhaps more—questions about prayer than when I first began to pray. My own experiences and those of others have not eliminated the struggle. Prayer does not come easily for me. I affirm that *prayer is mystery.*

But I cannot stop praying. Every time I try, I feel as if my soul is suffocating. I struggle with prayer, but it is a struggle for life. I am convinced that, outside of salvation itself, prayer is God's greatest gift to us. I believe it is the chief means of grace, and I agree with all those who have confessed that more things are wrought by prayer than this world ever dreams. The power and influence of prayer will only fully be known in eternity. I also affirm that *prayer is real.*

When I share the tension of these two affirmations, I find that some people are surprised. They assume that someone like me would not wrestle with prayer. They expect a prayer teacher to get beyond the questions and the perplexities and sail along in the life of prayer. But after their surprise subsides, they often say, "I'm so glad you said prayer is difficult for you. I feel the same way."

If what I have written thus far reflects your experience with prayer, this may be a book you have been looking for. It is not a primer on prayer. (For books that provide training in prayer, see the Suggested Reading on page 127.) But neither does this book give you permission to give up on prayer or to think that the best you can do is wander aimlessly in its practice. On the contrary, you will find here an invitation to pray that does not discount or pass judgment upon the questions and difficulties that accompany a serious prayer life. In the pages of this book,

I will ask you to roll up your sleeves and confront your problems with prayer—and then keep praying. As the title implies, sometimes you will feel as though you are talking in the dark. But the fact is, sound travels in both darkness and light.

PROLOGUE

You do not solve the mystery, you live the mystery.

—FREDERICK BUECHNER

Four hurricanes pounded Florida in 2004, leaving behind unprecedented paths of destruction. Three of the storms passed over our part of the state. And while our home sustained minor damage compared to so many others, Jeannie and I experienced the same anxieties as people around us. We all lived with uncertainty, sometimes for days. Each hurricane knocked out our electricity. When night fell, we found ourselves talking in the dark.

It's strange how hurricane-induced darkness differs from the darkness that comes every evening after sunset. As we sat in our little "safe room" or lay in bed, listening to the howling wind and rain, we found ourselves engulfed in a darkness as much internal as it was external. Questions about the strength of our house, the welfare of our neighbors, and our eventual outcome all went unanswered. Darkness yielded no clues and offered no guarantees.

Our experience with the hurricanes has become for me an analogy for exploring the mysteries of prayer. Sometimes we find ourselves "talking in the dark," and the darkness is neither fair nor friendly. It soaks into us, evoking old fears and raising new ones, exposing raw emotions and scary thoughts.

During the hurricanes, Jeannie and I prayed—as did millions of others. Some, like us, were largely spared. Others who called out to God lost everything. The only way you can dismiss that fact is to ignore it and push it deep down into your unconsciousness. But it does not lie there passively; it remains alive, and not in a good way. I've met a lot of people who, years later, still carry deep wounds from when they simply could not make sense out of things—including the knowledge that they prayed, but seemingly to no avail. When we feel like that, we cannot keep from asking, "What's going on?"

Ironically, the return of daylight didn't solve anything. The damage was already done. Light simply revealed the extent of the destruction. As Jeannie and I walked around the house and through the neighborhood, we made remarks like, "So *that's* what that loud crack was!" But being able to identify the damage did not eliminate it. In fact, the greater light only made us realize the severity of the situation and how long it would take to return to a sense of normalcy. When the electricity came back on and we could listen to the radio and watch television, the expanded awareness only broadened our understanding of how far-ranging the devastation was. Light revealed but did not heal.

Unfortunately, some literature about prayer is like that for me. It sheds light on the nature and practice of prayer, but in doing so it only makes the questions stand out more. Take healing prayer, for example. The more I learn about it, the more I wonder why some people for whom I pray have not been healed. Greater knowledge doesn't always improve the outlook or make it easier to handle. Most of the people I know who really struggle with prayer are those who have prayed—not those who sat around and philosophized about prayer, then dismissed it. The pains borne because of prayer come only when we pray. As we discovered during the hurricanes of 2004, you're pounded by the wind only when you're in the midst of the storm.

> YOU CAN HAVE A PRAYER LIFE AND CHOOSE TO AVOID THE MYSTERIES. OR YOU CAN INCLUDE THE MYSTERIES IN YOUR PRAYING, KNOWING THAT EVEN WHEN YOU DO, SOME WILL REMAIN.

If this approach to prayer is more than you want to deal with, now might be a good time to return this book and see if you can get a refund. It's not going to get any easier. Mysteries do not yield to quick fixes and simple formulas, and sometimes they never yield at all. Prayer is no different. You can have a prayer life and choose to avoid the mysteries. Or you can include the mysteries in your praying, knowing that even when you do, some will remain. This book is an expression of the latter choice. If that is what you want, read on.

Here's the simple truth: some prayers are answered, and some are not. Now, don't misunderstand me. I am not talking philosophically or theologically when I say that. I am merely making the statement based on my and others' observations and feelings about prayer. Some of you may want to shout, "God answers every prayer!" And you will add the often-cited three ways: yes, no, and not yet. Please do not read this paragraph as a frontal attack on that kind of thinking.

But do understand that I am not writing about what we may "think" or "believe" about prayer at this point. I'm merely trying to express the reality that we pray, and sometimes we do not get what we ask for. When this happens in the realm of insignificant matters, it doesn't make many waves. But when we stare into the face of unanswered prayer about deeply personal and extremely important concerns, the wear and tear on our souls is different.

When I move in this direction, I immediately think of Paul's thorn in the flesh (2 Cor. 12:7); C. S. Lewis's profound grief when his wife, Joy, died; and the parents of a young man killed in Iraq the day before he was to complete his tour of duty. How can we keep from asking in such moments, "What's the good of prayer?" We find ourselves talking in the dark. Most of what I write about in this book relates to that kind of darkness.

Resources abound for praying in the light. But what can we take with us into the darkness; what can we hold on to in the midst of it? One final warning: there's still time to turn back. But I hope you won't.

When the hurricanes were assaulting us and Jeannie and I talked in the darkness, we discovered (or rediscovered) the truth that sound travels in darkness just as much as it does in light. The noise of a hurricane can make talking more of an effort; the uncertainty can make conversation more challenging. But it does not affect the ability of sound to travel. I feel the same way about prayer. Many factors can make prayer more difficult and challenging, but we can talk in the dark days of our lives as surely as we can in the light-filled days. That is a central conviction of this book. If you can cling to it, what you are about to read may be what you've been looking for—and more importantly, maybe just what you need.

Long ago the prophet Jeremiah asked, "Is there no balm in Gilead? Is there no physician there?" (8:22). He wrote his lament when his nation was suffering greatly. Jeremiah's heart was broken, his face wet with tears. Of course, there was medicine in the land, and Israel had doctors. But the kind of care the nation needed went beyond the power of pills or persons. Likewise, we are never bereft of prayer, but we may need more than our customary views and practices of it. We may need to experience prayer in a new way—or more correctly, experience God in a new way. As one person said to me, "I want to know about the kind of prayer that will keep me praying when everything in me wants to quit." So do I. And I imagine you do as well.

PART ONE
FOUNDATIONS

I know the one in whom I have put my trust,
and I am sure that he is able
to guard until that day
what I have entrusted to him.

—2 TIMOTHY 1:12

God alone is the only One in Whom we can put our trust when we are uncertain about the way.

—DAVID MCKENNA

PRELUDE

TO PART ONE

Sometimes in prayer retreats I ask participants to write a prayer. It can be about anything currently affecting their lives. The only requirement is that the prayer be at least one page so it contains some detail. When people finish, I ask them to read back over their prayers in relation to these questions:

- What picture of God comes through in the prayer?
- What picture of yourself do you see in this prayer?
- How does the church show up in this prayer?
- What are the main emotions expressed?

I do not coerce any responses, but as participants are willing, I ask them to share insights from this exercise. The conversation is usually quite interesting.

Prayers flow from the well of deep belief. What we believe about God, ourselves, others, and the church comes through in the way we pray. The practice of prayer is rooted in our theology of prayer.

Part One is my attempt to develop a theology of prayer, but also one that does not evade the questions or minimize the struggle. Part One is my response to the man I mentioned in the introduction—the one who said he only wanted to know one thing: why he should keep praying.

CHAPTER 1

THE GOD PROBLEM

The best reason to pray is that God is really there. In praying, our unbelief gradually starts to melt. God moves smack into the middle of even an ordinary day. [God] is no longer someone we theorize about. [God] is someone we want to be near.

—EMILIE GRIFFIN

Let's face it: the number one problem we have with prayer is God. When our prayers seem to go unanswered, our first thought is, *Why didn't God answer?* We may have any number of related questions, but the primary one has to do with God. This is no different from other areas of life. When someone does not return our phone call or reply to our e-mail, we naturally wonder about the receiver. Since God is the receiver of our prayers, we naturally question God before we question anything else.

Between 1995 and 2003, Jeannie and I experienced the deaths of our last three parents. Her mother died in 1967 at age forty-two (when Jeannie was sixteen), and that was a "God problem" in its own right. In 1995 my mother died after a seven-month struggle with cancer. In 1997 Jeannie's dad died after a ten-day battle with a raging infection. And in 2003 my dad died after a four-year bout with Alzheimer's. During those eight years, we spent many days in doctors' offices, hospital rooms, waiting areas, and funeral homes. We slept in motels far from home and made decisions based on advice from people we didn't really know.

And we prayed . . . and prayed . . . and prayed. At the beginning of each parent's illness, we prayed for healing. In the middle of the suffering, we prayed for comfort. At the end, we prayed for release. Each parental death gave ample opportunities for our faith to be expressed—and tested. We experienced God's presence—and God's absence. We praised and we cried. But more than anything else, we felt as if we were riding a roller coaster. Some days it seemed God was receiving our prayers and responding. Other days it seemed God was receiving our prayers and ignoring them.

Over the years I have found that people will talk openly about similar experiences if they believe their spirituality or Christian commitment will not be judged or questioned. I've also discovered that when some people confess that their main problem with prayer is God, a lot of other thoughts and feelings that have never been processed—but left to dangle and fester—surface as well. A public face of faith, taken off, sometimes reveals a heart angry and broken by every attempt to make sense of circumstances. Most of the time, such folks admit they have never been told how to deal with these emotions, so all they know to do is "grin and bear it," which only ends up making matters worse. The Bible does not contain any verse that says, "Never let them see you sweat."

I was talking about this God problem in a prayer workshop in Indiana. A woman named Mary raised her hand and asked if she could share her experience. Almost immediately she began to cry. She told of how her husband came home from work one day with the news that his company was planning to promote him, but the promotion meant their family would have to move to another city. The entire family loved where they lived, and they had no prior warning that they might have to pull up roots. No one wanted to move, so Mary began to pray that God would somehow work out a way for her husband to get the promotion without having to leave town. But nothing changed. The move was imminent, and everyone was upset.

One evening after dinner, Mary was alone in the kitchen. Her husband had gone to the den to watch TV, and the children were in their rooms, doing homework. Without warning, a clot of frustration broke loose, and Mary heard herself say, "God, sometimes I hate you!" By this point in the story, she could hardly continue. She explained tearfully, "I honestly thought I was going to be struck dead on the spot. I was taught that you should never talk to God like that. But instead of dropping dead," she told us, "as soon as the words came out of my mouth, I felt something like warm oil running slowly from the top of my head all the way down to my feet. As it did so, warmth enveloped me, and an inner voice said, 'Mary, I know how you feel. And I love you.'" That transforming moment enabled her to make the move, but it also changed forever her feelings about prayer.

WE WRESTLE WITH GOD WHEN WHAT WE PRAY FOR DOESN'T HAPPEN.

Mary's story is not unique. We wrestle with God when what we pray for doesn't happen. And if enough frustration builds up, our "nice" prayers will erupt in silent or spoken prayers using words we're not even sure we are allowed to speak to God. I will never forget Mary's story, but as real as it was, it ended well. Not everyone's story does. I know there are others for whom things do not turn out all right. Some people are "stranded in the kitchen" without any transforming experience.

What's going on here? Surely more than we can ever put into words. But I think at the core is the fact that we wrestle with an invisible God. Praying to a God we cannot see is tremendously difficult. It's even challenging when we pray and get what we asked for. We still are not given an explanation of how our prayers were answered, and we are left to wonder if the same thing would have happened even if we had not prayed. And worse, when our prayers are not answered as we hoped, we can't make an appointment with God to find out why. In either case, talking to an invisible God keeps us dwelling in the land of mystery. We do not know how to live well in that land.

But if we are to continue praying, we must learn to live with mystery. If we cannot, eventually we will give up on prayer. Here are some questions that will never be answered:

- Why are some people healed while others aren't?
- Why do soldiers get killed the day before they are supposed to return home?
- Why does a young person die in an accident during a mission trip?
- Why does one person run late and miss boarding a plane that crashes, killing everyone else on board?

You can easily add your own questions to these. In fact, as time goes by, questions like these keep piling up, and no attempts to explain them away really do so.

The Bible has its own list of questions that were never fully answered. Job asked why righteous people suffer. The psalmist wondered why evil people prospered and good people didn't. Matthew surely must have wondered why every baby boy under age two had to die when Herod tried to kill the young Messiah. Paul prayed for God to remove his thorn in the flesh, but it remained. And even Jesus asked from the cross, "My God, my God, why have you forsaken me?"

Every "why?" passage in the Bible indicates that the person or group did not understand; they were living with mystery and had to pray in the midst of it. In fact, they wove *why?* into their praying. We must not miss that fact. We must ponder it as long as it takes for the truth to soak in. When we ask why in our prayers, we have somehow recognized that we are permitted to bring every question, every issue, every confusion, and every struggle to God. We may not understand what's going on, but God knows that we cannot pray authentically unless we can honestly express every thought and emotion. The old gospel song has it right—"what a privilege to carry everything to God in prayer!"[1]

In this regard, the apostle Thomas has become my hero. Many Christians have done him a great disservice by dubbing him "doubting Thomas" and considering him the kind of believer they do not want to be. On the contrary, he is precisely the kind of person we want to be when we don't understand what's going on. Thomas's acknowledgment of his doubt was the first step on his way back to God—not away from God. His honesty led him to make the strongest affirmation of faith in the New Testament: "My Lord and my God!" (John 20:28).

For Thomas, doubt was the tunnel that led from despair to hope. As long as we can pray our whys, we will not be paralyzed by mystery. And we will discover that prayer is not so much about getting answers as about gaining perspective.

This is a powerful idea, but there has to be more. We cannot live with mystery as the only reality we're dealing with. We must have some light. We call that light "revelation." The simple fact is, we can never know God through the power of our own reasoning, speculating, or calculating. The finite cannot understand the Infinite. So there must be a Story beyond our story—larger than our story, and a Story into which our story can be placed. There must be a more comprehensive view than our limited vision can provide. We cannot *think* our way into a perfect understanding of who God is. We must be told who God is—by God. And as Christians we believe we have been told in the pages of scripture.

In terms of prayer, this means we must not only pray our questions but also pray our faith. At some point we have to trust the revelation. In this regard, one of the great untapped strengths of prayer is the Trinity. To be sure, the Trinity is part of the mystery, for we will never be able to explain the exact relationship between the Father, Son, and Holy Spirit. But we do learn two essential truths from the Trinity: (1) God is a person, not a concept, and (2) each person of the Trinity reaches into creation to touch life and care for it.

The Father creates, then repeatedly enters the human scene to be with people and to deliver them. The Son lives on the earth as one who reached out every day of his life to touch others. And the Spirit has come to indwell us as we make our journey. Whatever else the Trinity is, the Godhead is not self-contained or self-satisfied. The Father, the Son, and the Spirit are all other-oriented. When life is unfair, we are propelled to ask, "Does God understand? Does God care? Does God help?" All three persons of the Trinity respond with a divine "Yes." The fact that God is a person means God understands. All three persons of the Trinity show that God cares, and all three reveal significant ways God helps. The Trinity takes us into God's heart even when we cannot understand God's ways. The most important truth we know about God's heart is that it is a heart of love.

But there is a downside. The more we believe that God's heart is loving, the more we wonder why God doesn't intervene more often than it seems, especially when our prayer for God to do so is totally appropriate. We feel kinship with Lazarus's sister, Martha, who went out to meet Jesus on his way to their house and said forthrightly, "If you had been here, my brother would not have died" (John 11:21). When life is unfair, we cannot keep from asking a loving God, "Where were you? Why didn't you come in time?" To claim there are any easy answers to those questions would be to lie.

On the other hand, there is revelation. And that is why we can never develop an adequate theology of prayer or a meaningful practice of prayer apart from a serious, sustained study of scripture. The Bible keeps us from drowning in our own speculations. Revelation is what makes us pilgrims instead of wanderers. Wanderers have no map. They may be searching for something but have no way to tell whether moving in one direction is better than another. Pilgrims, on the other hand, walk a journey that may include darkness as well as light, but at least they have a compass. Revelation does not eliminate the mystery, but it puts mystery in a different context. That context is too large to describe in a few words, but I think it's fair to say that the overarching Story is God's declaration, "I am with you—I will never leave you or forsake you."

This is the revelation, but with only that, we do not address the God problem. To know that something is true is a step in the right direction, but until that truth becomes real and active in our lives, it resembles a concept more than an experience. We need more than revelation to deal with the God problem; we need presence. If God stays safely detached from our lives, it really doesn't matter who God is or what the Bible says about God. For anything to be markedly different, we must have what others have called "the Presence."

Do you remember when, as a child, you had to enter a strange place—maybe even a scary place? Perhaps you said something like this to a parent: "I'll go if you'll go with me." To know your parent loved you was not enough; you wanted presence. The same holds true for God. Knowing that God is love is not enough. We need Presence, and that is precisely what God offers. As Father, God has come again and again to deliver us from evil. When Jesus was born, Joseph was told to name the child Emmanuel, which means "God with us." And through the Holy Spirit, God continues to be with us when life is unfair. In fact, the Holy Spirit prays for us when we do not know how to pray for ourselves. Paul put it this way: "The Spirit helps us in our weakness; for we do not know how to pray as we ought, but that very Spirit intercedes with sighs

KNOWING THAT GOD IS LOVE IS NOT ENOUGH. WE NEED PRESENCE, AND THAT IS PRECISELY WHAT GOD OFFERS.

too deep for words" (Rom. 8:26). To fully describe the presence of God is beyond my ability or the scope of this book. But I do want to refer to it in three significant ways.

God is with us as a *conquering* presence. We all have heard stories of God's supernatural action to stop evil, heal disease, and so forth. Many of you reading this book can testify that God is able to do far more than we can ask or imagine. I always encourage people to pray for God to be present as the One who can overcome anything. God's intervention does happen, and sometimes it seems to happen in response to prayer. My friend Maxie Dunnam has stared into the mystery and asked an intriguing question: "What if there are some things God either cannot or will not do until and unless we pray?"[2] So, never fail to pray for God to come as conqueror.

But again, what we pray for doesn't always happen. Sometimes we are not healed. Sometimes those we love are not restored. Soldiers we've prayed for sometimes do not come home. Weekly prayer meetings have to deal with unanswered requests. Is God no longer present—or is there more to God's presence than conquering? The Bible says there is more. The second dimension is *comfort*. God takes seriously this aspect of presence, and so must we. In fact, the Holy Spirit is often called the Comforter. And the saints of the ages witness to the power and benefit of the Spirit's comfort.

If we are to take seriously God's comfort, we must first understand what kind of comfort God provides. We need more than the contemporary understanding of comfort, which usually links comfort with consolation. Consolation is nothing to minimize, and most of us can tell wonderful stories of times when God's presence brought a peace that exceeded all understanding. But the word *comfort* means more than that. It comes from the Latin word *fortis*, the word from which we get the English word *fortify*. Comfort means more than a state of peace; it also signifies strength. When God is present as Comforter, God strengthens by giving the ability to cope with whatever is happening. David demonstrated this understanding of comfort in the Twenty-third Psalm: "Even though I walk through the darkest valley, I fear no evil; for you are with me; your rod and your staff—they comfort me" (v. 4).

When I took physics in high school, I learned about "equal but opposite pressure." I remember Dr. Gerald McCoy holding an empty aluminum can and rather easily crushing it before our eyes. Then he filled another can with water. He could not crush it with one hand. The water inside the can exerted a pressure equal but opposite to the force pressing in from the outside. I view that demonstration as a parable of how God's presence comforts us. The Spirit fills us with a power that is equal and opposite to the force pressing upon us. And the Bible takes such comfort a step farther, declaring, "The one who is in you is greater than the one who is in the world" (1 John 4:4).

But there are times when the outside pressure collapses us and those around us. Not every enemy is defeated. Not every sick person is healed. The Bible clearly indicates that we live in a world where good and evil coexist, and sometimes evil gets the final say—or does it? Does God's presence have anything to say about that? I believe so, and that brings us to the third dimension: God's *clarifying* presence.

Even when problems remain unsolved and death triumphs over life, we must not overlook one final idea. The longest life we've ever heard of is less than the snap of a finger in time compared to eternity. Some in our day would call this pie-in-the-sky Christianity. Christians call it perspective. Some would say that to include this view of time as a form of God's comfort is to become escapists. Christians say it is nothing other than including all of life in the story of how God deals with us. Is earth the only terrain where God can work? Is God's power to right wrongs, heal diseases, and solve problems limited to humans' life span? By no means! God's comfort includes eternity as well as the here and now. The Bible puts it this way: "For this slight momentary affliction is preparing us for an eternal weight of glory beyond all measure, because we look not at what can be seen but at what cannot be seen; for what can be seen is temporary, but what cannot be seen is eternal" (2 Cor. 4:17-18).

"What can be seen" includes the bad as well as the good. And the Bible makes clear that no matter what is going on in our lives, it is but a slight, momentary affliction compared to what our eternal lives will be like. This does not mean that Christians grieve less, but it does mean we do not grieve as those who have no hope. The grave does not have the last word; God does. And that word shouts to all who will hear it that there is going to be a new heaven and a new earth where "death will be no more; mourning and crying and pain will be no more" (Rev. 21:4). God's clarifying presence helps us to pray against the backdrop of eternity. And there are times when that is the only way we can pray.

Revelation and presence enable us to move back and forth along the spectrum of mystery and certainty. As we do so, we discover another element that helps us face the God problem: grace. In relation to prayer, grace has significant messages to convey. Grace says, "You are not alone, and you are not limited to your own power to deal with what comes to you in life." And with grace, somehow we make it. Because God loves everyone, grace is not limited to believers. But believers know better how to recognize grace, respond to it, and give thanks for it. *Grace* is the word that tells us that God knows life is too big for us to handle. Ego may want us to believe we can handle it, but in the furnace of adversity, ego melts into presumption. Grace is the way we experience and apply God's revelation and presence.

The God problem never completely resolves itself. The last step is always trust. We walk by faith, not by sight. But faith is not guesswork or baseless hope. It is not insanity. Praying in the face of mystery is not what wild and crazy people do. Praying by faith is in the spirit described by my friend Dr. Ken Kinghorn: "Faith completes the trend of available evidence." And the available evidence is that sometimes God conquers, God comforts, and God clarifies. We pray in relation to each of those realities.

Sometimes our prayer feels like what I've come to call "isometric praying"—having to push against things that do not budge. Prayer is hard, frustrating work. Isometric praying goes against the notion that if we push something, it ought to move. It surely undercuts the notion that we are the masters of our fate. But such praying is one of the ways we build spiritual muscle and become stronger and better able to face the unfairness of life. If we continue to pray even in the face of the God problem, we will discover truths about God and ourselves that we could not learn any other way. Most of all, we will find that we are not alone.

CHAPTER 2
THE HUMAN PROBLEM

Since we're only human, understanding God is out of the question.
But trusting [God] is not.

—Marie T. Freeman

Watching our children learn to walk was both a joyful and a frightening experience for Jeannie and me. We were happy to see them reach this developmental milestone. After crawling their way along in a walker's world, they decided to join the rest of us. But we also watched anxiously as they fell over and over again. Whoever said it's a miracle anyone lives to be three years old wasn't exaggerating! Even though our children came within centimeters of knocking their brains out, we stood by, encouraging them to get up and keep trying. For every fall we said, "That's okay. Get up. You can do it." And eventually they did. In fact, they became so good at walking that they don't remember those moments we will never forget.

Prayer is like that. All sorts of human problems are connected to it. But God delights to see us keep trying. Often we come close to knocking our souls out, and once in a while we slam into the "sharp objects" of life and require attention. But the Holy Spirit keeps saying, "That's okay. Get up. You can do it." Long ago, the apostle Paul described it this way in the book of Romans: "God's Spirit is right alongside helping us along. If we don't know how or what to pray, it doesn't matter. [The Spirit] does our praying in and for us, making prayer out of our wordless sighs, our aching groans" (8:26, *The Message*).

If we are to keep talking in the dark, we must face the human problem as well as the God problem. And like the God problem, many dimensions of the human problem are hidden in the cloud of mystery. I've already told you that after more than forty years of praying, I still do not understand prayer. I get up many mornings and go to my place of devotion with no sense that my praying makes any difference. This does not mean that I go there reluctantly or discouraged; it simply means I go there realizing that prayer will always be bigger than me and beyond me. I pray realizing that I am not the one in charge. I also find that the older I get, the more content I am to leave some situations in the realm of mystery and wonder.

At the same time, not everything about the human problem lies beyond understanding or description. In this chapter I will examine some of the things I believe we can deal with in the human dimension.

I begin with a pair of opposites: underselling and overselling prayer. I deal with them together because I believe they spring from the same source. Either of them happens because we do not study prayer enough to know what the Bible teaches about it. Truth be told, we start with our own ideas and then add a few sketchy verses about prayer, thinking that the result will be an adequate theology of prayer. We have not done our homework before we try to do our headwork. We have grounded our beliefs about prayer in our own reasoning, rather than in God's revelation.

The ability to quote scriptures about prayer does not mean we have rooted our understanding about prayer in the Bible. And without the reference point of revelation, we can easily pitch prayer too high or too low. When we pitch it too high, we create unrealistic expectations; when we pitch it too low, we leave the impression that it doesn't matter much whether we pray. In either case, prayer is damaged—prayer is caricatured and perhaps even counterfeited. Overselling and underselling are the extremes to avoid. In between are other significant issues to deal with.

One problem is the notion that prayer is magic. Many people believe that if they use the right words in the right way and with the right spirit, God is obligated to answer in the way they have requested. Frankly, this is pagan prayer, not Christian prayer. One of the best examples of pagan prayer occurs in 1 Kings 18:16-39, when Elijah confronts the prophets of Baal at Mount Carmel to determine who is the true God. Prayer resides at the heart of the encounter. Elijah lets the prophets of Baal go first. They pray "magic" prayers, using all their incantations properly and praying passionately from morning until noon. When nothing happens, they pray louder and even slash themselves so that their blood flowed. All this elaborate ritual continues until evening, but Baal does not respond. The Bible says, "No one answered, no one paid attention" (v. 29, NIV).

When Elijah's turn comes, all the emotion, incantations, and lengthiness are replaced by one simple prayer (vv. 36-37), and God answers immediately, leaving no doubt about who is the true God. The story is as ancient as the Hebrew scriptures and as modern as last week's worship service. Magic conditions us to think, *We did what we were supposed to do; now God is obligated to do what we asked.* Magic creates the false belief that we have prayed sincerely, correctly, and repeatedly—now God must respond accordingly. Prayer becomes a formula, and the purpose of prayer is to get results. Such prayer is a transaction, not a relationship. And worse, it is a relationship we initiate in a way that requires God to honor the contract.

Let me be very clear about this kind of prayer. It is not restricted to one particular style of praying. We may pray using ritual and liturgy, or pray spontaneously and even in an unknown tongue; yet the notion of what we are doing can be "magical." We don't notice that it's magic when, in fact, God comes through in the way we asked or expected. It's only when our prayer doesn't get results that we are left to wonder what happened. And if we are using prayer magically, our only option is to conclude that we didn't pray sincerely, correctly, or long enough. Prayer turns into a kind of spiritual mathematics, leaving us to deduce that if we had asked more people to pray, spent more time praying, or had more faith, the outcome would have been different.

I witnessed this thinking about prayer when the son of some dear friends suffered with leukemia for years, going into and out of remission. Probably not a day went by without someone, in addition to Timmy's mother and father, praying for Timmy's healing. I prayed often myself and participated in small-group and congregational prayer. More than once we anointed Timmy with oil and laid hands on him. But Timmy eventually died. At the funeral home, someone approached Timmy's mother and said, "You know, it's so unfortunate. If you had just had more faith, he wouldn't have died." That person's understanding of prayer angered me then, and it still does. Who could possibly want a child to be healed more than a parent? Who could have done anything more than Timmy's mother and father did—for years? No one. And no amount of spiritualizing will explain the mystery.

Magic prayer also creates a market for "prayer experts" who can either teach you how to get results or do your praying for you. Their products and toll-free numbers are always available. This has nothing to do with legitimate intercession by others on our behalf, or the fact that we do benefit from the sincere prayers of brothers and sisters in Christ. Rather, it is the mistaken notion that somewhere there are a handful of people who "really know" about prayer and how to pray—that a relatively small inner circle of "the illuminati" can get the results we are unable to get for ourselves. The problem is, when we face life's greatest challenges, we do not need gurus; we need God.

WHEN WE FACE LIFE'S GREATEST CHALLENGES, WE DON'T NEED GURUS; WE NEED GOD.

I have studied the Bible thoroughly on this topic, and there is not one hint that prayer is magical, not one indication that you need the help of an expert to be able to pray as you should. Every teaching about prayer in the Old and New Testaments is a teaching you can put into practice. When Jesus gave the Lord's Prayer to the apostles, he did not indicate that he should do their praying for them. Instead, he prefaced the prayer by saying, "*When* you pray." Again, this is not a rejection of corporate prayer. It is not a prohibition against healing services. It is simply the denial that prayer is magic.

The Bible invites others to join us in prayer, but it never portrays them as having an inside track on prayer or secret knowledge about it. I think Jesus attacked ideas about magic—whether regarding prayer or other matters—when he commended the faith of a mustard seed (Matt. 17:20). I have experienced times in my life when my faith was weak, and I needed others to carry me into the presence of God with their intercessions. I have had times when, like men and women in the Bible, I called on the church to pray. But my faith in prayer was never smaller than a mustard seed. That reminds me that no matter how I feel about prayer at any given moment, I am still called to pray. My prayer is never "too small" to get God's attention.

Rather than resorting to magic, take heart! Even prayers as simple as "help" and "thanks" reach God. This is not an excuse to do the least we can do when we pray; it is simply a reminder that in our weakest moments, God hears.

Another problem is viewing prayer as prevention. This is the idea that we can surround people with a kind of "spiritual bubble" wherein they will be safe. I believe in the protective power of prayer to a certain extent. I believe that when we get to heaven, we will be amazed to see how we benefited from the Lord's Prayer—how often God led us away from temptation and delivered us from evil. Therefore, I pray that God will protect me and others. The trouble is, I know people who prayed that their loved ones would return home safely, only to have them return home in a casket. There seems to be no way to predict—much less determine—why protective prayer seems to work one time but not another. In the mystery of this prayer, I would counsel you to keep praying for God's protection, but I also caution you not to view such praying as a guarantee that everything will turn out fine.

What's going on here? I've already alluded to mystery, but I don't believe that's the whole story. We also have to factor in the reality of the Fall. By the time we get to the third chapter in the Bible, something has gone radically wrong with the whole creation. Life as God intended it has already essentially derailed. The rest of the Bible contains the story of life that is completely and cosmically deformed. Prayer has not escaped its own contamination. Nothing and no one has.

We do not live in Eden, and no amount of effort will re-create it. I will never understand how prayer has been affected by the Fall, but it has. I've read hundreds of books on prayer and visited with respected prayer teachers and theologians about this very problem. No one has the last word. But it does seem clear that the God-human relationship has been thoroughly messed up. Communication between God and us has been affected as well. This being so, it leaves us without having to believe that either God or we "failed" in the prayer relationship. God is not capricious, and we are not disinterested.

We practice imperfect prayer in a fallen world. We can't escape that fact. It's one of the reasons the Bible teaches that a new heaven and a new earth will be necessary for God to repair life from the destructive effects of the Fall. Until then, sickness and sorrow, pain and death, will be part of the picture—and no amount of prayer will stop their effects every time. I keep reminding myself that the second time Lazarus died, he stayed in the grave. Every person I have prayed for over the years who was protected or preserved by God eventually will die. This is not fatalism but reality. If I knew everything, I could select when, how, and for whom to pray. But since I don't, my call is to pray the Lord's Prayer at all times—and to believe that this prayer never falls on deaf divine ears.

Now we're ready to confront what may be the chief human problem: second-guessing God or ourselves. I have alluded to this issue already, but now I want to deal with it specifically. Whether our prayers are answered as we hope, we must never try to explain prayer. I learned this from one of my main prayer mentors, Dr. Tom Carruth. One day in a seminary class, he warned us never to presume that just because a prayer gets answered, our prayer is the one God has responded to. We never know who else might have been praying. He also cautioned us not to assume that it is our fault when a prayer goes unanswered. We do not evaluate prayer by how clearly we can see what's happening. As Brennan Manning has repeated on numerous occasions, the only thing we can hold on to is ruthless trust.

> THE FINAL CHALLENGE IS NOT TO STUDY PRAYER BUT TO PRACTICE IT AS A MEANS OF GRACE.

But how do I know if I am trusting? One sign is that I am willing to change the question from "Why me?" to "How me?" I have never known a single person who prayed better by analyzing prayer. The final challenge is not to study prayer but to practice it as a means of grace. Loss, pain, suffering, and death are part of living in this world. If we are healthy, we never invite these things on ourselves or others. They always come as intruders, and often with little or no warning. Yesterday we were well; today we are sick. An hour ago we were happy; after the phone call, we are grieving. Last week we had a job; today we are unemployed.

If we limit our praying to the question, "Why me?" we will be pulled into a philosophical black hole. Anger and confusion will suck the life out of us and hurl us into the pit of despair. But if we pray, "How me?" we will find ourselves on a different path. This is not succumbing to realities we cannot change; it is choosing to live in the midst of them. This is not fatalism but faith. When we pray, "How me?" we deliberately choose to reframe the picture and focus on our disappointment in relation to the context of eternity.

I must be very careful here. I have seen devout Christians suffer greatly. I have watched life turn devoted disciples inside out. Christianity is not an immunization against disease; it is an insight into life when we are afflicted. We may get hurt, cry out, or become depressed. But we do this as those who believe in a God who is really present, and that our misfortunes matter to him. We cannot escape "the valley of the shadow of death" (Ps. 23:4, NIV), but we do not have to walk through it alone. For reasons we can never fully understand, God may not provide what we ask for, but God will never be absent when we ask for God's presence.

At this point, we enter into another human problem in prayer: artificiality. Unfortunately, some of us believe the only way to be a good Christian witness is to put on a happy face to hide the depth of pain we feel when life is unfair. When we do this, we create two serious problems. First, we segment our lives in a way that keeps God from working at the deepest level of our experiences and needs. Superficial prayer is as far as we're willing to let God go, and we get what we pray for. And second, we project a false image of reality to others. By pretending to be okay when we aren't, we mislead people into thinking they will be okay when the winds of life blow against them. When they experience hardship and feel terrible, they conclude that God must have answered our prayers but not theirs. So, we not only put a lid on our deepest needs; we create an illusion that will only damage others' faith when they encounter hard times in their lives. We have no permission whatsoever to be artificial in our praying.

I was privileged to know Arnold Prater, a well-known United Methodist pastor and evangelist. More than anyone else, he helped me see the danger of artificial praying. In a sermon he told about a pattern of unrealistic prayer that had developed in his morning devotions. Each day he would get up, go to his place of prayer, and begin to exude flowery words like these: "O thou omnipotent God, who dwellest in splendor and who reignest in glory from age to age," and so on. Arnold said he could almost hear God's fingers drumming on the banister of heaven, communicating God's boredom with his artificial praying. One morning, Arnold reached a turning point; he moved into real prayer. He woke up with a two-Excedrin headache. Holding his head as he stumbled to his place of prayer, all he could say that morning was, "God . . . my head hurts!" In that moment, Arnold heard the voice of God deep in his soul saying, "Well, Arnold—finally! Now you know how to pray."

Living in Orlando, headquarters of Campus Crusade for Christ, I had the opportunity to follow Bill Bright's journey from the day he was diagnosed with pulmonary fibrosis to the day he died. I saw Bill once before he died, and he spoke honestly about his condition and confidently about his faith in God. I was impressed with the way he blended reality and trust. We will never know how many millions of people interceded for Bill Bright, and surely no one did so more deeply than his wife, Vonette. From time to time, the news media gave updates about his condition, and they were not good. Only after his death did we discover that he had been writing a book about preparing to die.

Vonette gave Jeannie and me a copy of Bill's book, *The Journey Home: Finishing with Joy*. I read it immediately, and it will bless me for the rest of my life. It was Bill Bright's account of what it was like to die a painful death at the hand of a relentless disease—and to do so as a Christian. He pulled no punches and never glossed over his feelings. But Bill Bright's feelings were not his faith; the realities could not eclipse the revelation. He called his experience "joy in perspective." Perhaps as nearly as any other phrase I could choose, that is what I have tried to describe in this chapter. This is the reality of how people of faith deal with the human problems of prayer—with ruthless trust.

The joy comes in knowing that disease and death do not have the final word; God does. Perspective comes in knowing that no matter how much we cannot understand and no matter how much we suffer, eternity is real and ultimately the defining element. Joy in perspective does not force us to hide any emotion, nor does it force us to abandon faith. We cannot eliminate the human problem in prayer, but we can find grace to live with it, until we reach the day when even the last enemy—death—will be swallowed up in victory.

CHAPTER 3

THE CHURCH PROBLEM

Most of us would like to think, or simply assume, that our church is a house of prayer because it is a church that prays. But is it really a house of prayer? What did Jesus mean by that? What does a praying church look like?

—JONATHAN GRAF

When it comes to prayer, we like to think the church would do us more good than harm. But that is not always the case. Sometimes the church amplifies both the God problem and the human problem. Although I do not like to admit it, when confronting the problems associated with prayer, we have to include the church.

I've been involved in prayer ministry for more than thirty years. I've led prayer retreats and workshops in all sorts of locations. Often people say, "We have never had anything like this in our church." Newcomers and old-timers alike often cannot recall ever having a prayer emphasis in their congregation. And in some places, people are hard-pressed to remember the last sermon or lesson on prayer. Yet churches say prayers all the time, on all occasions, but many rarely provide any sustained or progressive instruction in prayer itself. This leaves the body of Christ vulnerable to specific and significant dangers.

Perhaps most of all, the church has succumbed to acculturation in regard to prayer. We have adapted prayer to prevailing notions in society rather than practicing prayer in relation to biblical principles. We end up with counterfeit and caricatured prayer—often without even realizing we've done so. It particularly happens both in underselling and overselling prayer.

We undersell prayer through our silence about it. For congregations to go for years—in some cases, decades—with no intentional and sustained teaching about prayer leaves people adrift in developing their prayer lives. The result is that people do not mature or grow stronger in prayer. A man told me honestly during a prayer retreat, "I don't pray any better than when I first began to pray." He had received absolutely no help or guidance in nurturing his prayer life.

It is not unusual for prayer times on Sunday morning or prayer meetings on Wednesday night to sound like broken records as the same concerns are prayed for, often by the same people and in the same ways. Nothing ever changes; it's only repeated. If you were a nonbeliever going to some churches, you'd get the idea that prayer only has to do with

getting well when you're sick,
being safe when you travel,
or having success when you try something.

While these matters are important and surely have their place in prayer, they do not begin to address the full range of life issues that can be expressed prayerfully. In fact, repeating such requests over and over, week after week, may mask the things people really need to be praying about.

By keeping prayer limited to a few selected subjects expressed in predictable ways, we undersell it by reducing it to little more than spiritualized psychology. Prayer becomes the church's way to help people feel better about themselves and have a more positive attitude about their lives. And when it comes to intercessory prayer, we can be lulled into the spiritual sleep of believing we have done everything we are supposed to do for others once we have prayed for them. To whatever extent we are tempted to undersell prayer in ways like these, we have become removed from the robust life of prayer. There is no ascending into profound praise or any descent into wrestling with principalities and powers. Prayer remains contained, comfortable, and controlled.

But underselling prayer has a twin: overselling it. In North American Christianity, one of the ways we do this is by teaching that prayer guarantees God will act in certain ways so that we can receive what we ask for. Prayer becomes a manipulative tactic we try on God. The undertone of such prayer becomes, "Okay, God, we've prayed; now you must answer—and answer when and how we say." When such an attitude prevails, prayer as ruthless trust and abandonment to divine providence gets lost under a pile of "have it your way" expressions. Such prayer keeps our idolized "Self" at the center, even though our prayer language makes it seem that we want God to be sovereign.

This kind of praying fits right into our culture's obsession with a value system based on consumerism, success, a growing economy, and a pervasive prosperity unlike most other places in the world today. We are so anesthetized by this kind of prayer that we hardly realize it is being defined and directed more by the gross national product than by scripture. And failing to realize this, we continue to oversell prayer in ways that create people who can teach Sunday school classes one day and engage in immoral business practices the next. When the bottom line is "getting blessed," prayer can easily exist alongside any means to achieve the blessing.

Another prayer problem in the church is assumption. We assume that prayer is "natural" and therefore so intrinsic to our nature that everyone will pray—and pray well. So the church doesn't feel the need to teach about prayer any more than it feels a need to teach about breathing. We assume that if God made us to pray, we will pray. On one level this is true. I have yet to meet a person—Christian or not—who has told me that he or she has never prayed. In a sense, prayer is natural and we were made to pray. But to allow that assumption to cause us to avoid intentional and sustained training about prayer is a mistake.

I HAVE YET TO MEET A PERSON—CHRISTIAN OR NOT—WHO HAS TOLD ME THAT HE OR SHE HAS NEVER PRAYED.

I propose a change of view. Rather than assuming that prayer is like breathing, let's assume it is like talking. Talking is natural. We are made to talk. Parents eagerly await the day when their children begin making sounds and trying to say words. Often they write their child's first word into his or her baby book, never to be forgotten. And on the day the child says that first word, the parents call or e-mail friends and family members to let them know that the child has spoken a real word. But no parent stops there. No parent says, "Well, I'm glad that finally happened. Now we can move on to other things. My child is talking." On the contrary, a child's first word ignites an entire process that leads the child farther into the experience of speech. For the rest of his or her life, assuming normal development, the child will learn to talk better.

I believe that much of the church problem regarding prayer could be solved if we viewed prayer as speech. We would celebrate every person's entry into the world of prayer, but we would connect our celebration with never-ending guidance for praying better. When one of the apostles asked Jesus to teach them to pray, he was not asking how to begin praying. The disciples had already done that. He was asking Jesus to teach them how to pray more deeply and meaningfully. Doubtless, Jesus celebrated that his friends had prayed previously, and he knew they were made for prayer. But he did not stop there. By example and instruction, he enrolled them in the school of prayer—and never announced a graduation day.

When we in the church teach people how to deepen their prayer lives, we put ourselves in a position to deal with the problem of acculturation. We could actually undertake a serious study on the biblical theology of prayer. We could teach prayer in a celebrative atmosphere without creating the impression that only "prayer warriors" know how to really pray. We could deal with the stutterings and stammerings that accompany anyone's prayer life. We could help people establish and expand a rich prayer vocabulary. We could show that people of differing personalities and preferences can all pray authentically. We could establish concrete prayer ministries where the crossroads of Christ and culture intersect, confronting the principalities and powers with divine power that can fulfill our desire for God's kingdom to come and God's will to be done, on earth as it is in heaven.

But we are not likely to do this if we view prayer as breathing. With this view we will continue to limp along, content with the knowledge that "everyone is praying" and assuming that all are praying well—or at least well enough. Acculturation will win the day. Misleading models will remain—sometimes in the public eye—and prayer will become another expression of "privatized spirituality" that has already captured too much of the American soul.

And yet it does not have to be that way. Church is the very place where prayer can come alive. This is all the more true and necessary if we believe that prayer is natural but has to be cultivated—like talking. If prayer sometimes feels like talking in the dark, the church must be a hand we can touch in that darkness. But what would this mean?

Jesus provided guidance when he said that the Temple in Jerusalem was intended to be a "house of prayer" (Matt. 21:13). For Christians, the church serves as that house, and the image of a house is one of totality. Beyond specific and limited times of prayer in worship, midweek prayer services, prayerful administrative meetings, prayer groups, and private devotions, the church must create an environment of prayer in all it does, and it must encourage people to bring all of their lives under the purview of prayer. Dr. Tom Carruth called it "total prayer for total living." It is a view of prayer more as a way of life than as a time. This perspective will mean an increase in the amount of praying we do, but more than that, it will mean a growing sense that we live in an atmosphere of prayer—an atmosphere in which the Spirit helps us in our weakness by praying for us in ways that go beyond the words we are able to say.

When I speak about prayerful living in workshops, I often have to clarify that I am not advocating any reduction in actual praying. This would make no more sense than if a chef were to say, "I live in an atmosphere of food, so I never have to stop and eat." We would read that person's obituary in a couple of weeks. Of course, there are times for personal and corporate prayer. But these acts and occasions must arise from a more pervasive prayerfulness. An environment of prayer means that God is the reference point, not us. What God is doing—not what we are doing—is of utmost importance. We live, move, and have our being in God.

Jesus modeled prayerful living for us. He observed fixed times of personal prayer and participated in synagogue worship services where specific prayers were offered. But he also moved through the day in communion with God, able to move into and out of prayer with such ease that it appeared he was in a spirit of prayer all the time. Speaking with God and speaking with others was a singular experience. Jesus was attentive to God, on his knees and on his feet. As the body of Christ, the church needs to model and commend this kind of praying. When we do, as happened in the book of Acts, people will be able to tell that we have been with Jesus.

JESUS WAS ATTENTIVE TO GOD, ON HIS KNEES AND ON HIS FEET.

To develop a prayerful atmosphere takes time, and it is achieved in stages—just as with learning to talk. No congregation will do prayer ministry exactly like any other one, for no two churches are alike. The fact is, many congregations have neglected intentional prayer ministry for so long that they could start just about anywhere and it would be a step forward. But at the same time, I am happy to tell you that prayer ministry in the local church is one of the dimensions of healthy congregational life receiving fresh attention. On one occasion, I heard Dr. Lyle

Schaller say that the position of "prayer minister" (usually a volunteer layperson) is the fastest-growing position in churches today. Thanks to the Internet, many congregations have ongoing intercessory prayer ministries as faithful men and women receive and transmit requests. Jeannie and I are blessed to be part of a church with a vibrant prayer ministry.

But most of all, if we knew how willing the risen Christ is to help us live a life of total prayer, we would run to him and ask him to deal decisively with us individually and collectively until the church becomes what it is meant to be. We would practice our discipleship in relation to prayer. The root meaning of *disciple* is "learner." We would say with the first apostles, "Lord, teach us to pray" (Luke 11:1). We would open ourselves to his instruction and seek for the best resources possible to help us confront the church problem. To make this commitment is to step into the stream of what the Spirit is doing to renew the body of Christ and to make the church once again a "house of prayer."

CHAPTER 4
NEVERTHELESS!

I shall cling to the rope God has thrown me,
even if my numb hands can no longer feel it.

—Sophie Scholl

In the face of the problems we've examined, we have three choices related to prayer: (1) to stop praying; (2) to keep praying, but with diminished commitment; or (3) to stay at our prayer post and continue to pray as best we can. I have known some people who made the first choice, and quite a few others who made the second choice. I'm writing this chapter to encourage you to make the third choice. That choice is not quick or easy. The mystery, questions, and confusion that swirl around prayer are real and formidable. Life has the power to make us stumble and, sometimes, to knock us off our feet. When life doesn't make sense, we have to decide what we will do about prayer.

For Christians, the decision revolves around the second or third choices—whether to make prayer a matter of "saying the right words" but without much conviction or confidence, or to do our best to continue praying earnestly and authentically. There is a form of prayer that sounds good but does little good. It is prayer set on "automatic pilot"—prayer that goes through the motions but is itself motionless. I have prayed like this at times in my life. I was not willing to give up the appearance of praying, but I was largely unsure about what good my prayers were accomplishing. I know what it is to feel the emptiness of prayer. It is a place where I have been but did not want to stay.

Moving out of such praying is possible when we add one word to our prayer vocabulary: *nevertheless.* At first glance, the word may not seem to add much to our prayer lives. But I am convinced it is the bridge word that enables us to cross over the chasm of doubt that can so easily separate superficial and substantive praying. It is a word that fuels the soul for a return to meaningful prayer. It is the word that will keep us talking in the dark.

You may already be ahead of me on this, but I discovered the power of *nevertheless* when I saw its significance for Jesus when he prayed in the garden of Gethsemane. I had read the story many times before. Most of the time I focused on Jesus' abandonment to God: "not what I want but what you want." That's an impressive quality, and it lies at the heart of radical discipleship. Abandonment is one of the big actions for any believer. But one day I realized that the impressive phrase is preceded by the word *nevertheless.*

I stopped in my tracks.

Nevertheless what? Nevertheless why? Nevertheless how? Nevertheless who? Nevertheless when? All these questions rose up to consume my devotional attentiveness and made me realize I had skimmed over the word that makes the rest of the sentence so powerful. Here was the Son of God, coming to his greatest moment of struggle and choosing to make it an occasion of prayer—but prayer that was uttered only in relation to other matters. "Nevertheless" means there were other things going on inside and around Jesus—things that could have taken him in completely different directions. It was night, and he was talking in the dark. And in that situation his prayer was salvaged by the single word: *nevertheless*. What did this mean for Jesus? What does it mean for us?

First, *"nevertheless" praying keeps us from ignoring reality.* "Nevertheless" takes reality fully into account. It does not ignore the feelings, sidestep the questions, or gloss over the circumstances. But neither does it allow those things to have the last word or the power to shut us down. When we pray "nevertheless" prayers, we declare to ourselves and those around us that our lives have more than a past and a present—they also have a future. The final word has not yet been spoken.

I have known people who were overwhelmed by the downsides of human experience, but their spirits were not consumed. They had a "nevertheless" left inside them, and its power enabled them to bear their suffering and eventually rise above it. Later in this book, I will tell you about some of them. They are real people who prayed in the midst of the worst circumstances life could hurl at them. They were not able to do this because of positive thinking but because of profound faith. Such praying is not so much explained as it is experienced.

People have said to me, "I don't know how they can bear up under what they are going through. I'm not sure I could stand it." And they are exactly right. When life is going well for us, we do not have to depend on capacities intended only for those going through deep waters. When the sun is shining, we don't need to have every light on in the house. But when the darkness overtakes us, a certain grace comes to illuminate our way. There is a quality of life given to us when we must face terrible situations and deal with circumstances we cannot change. When we pray "nevertheless," we affirm that faith.

> THE INCARNATION OF JESUS IS THE SUPREME "NEVERTHELESS."

The incarnation of Jesus is the supreme "nevertheless." Christ came to a fallen world, and his advent did not immediately change the world. Some would argue that when Jesus came into the world, evil reared its ugly head even more to cause people to prefer darkness to light. His teachings and actions, marvelous as they were, did not fundamentally alter the sinfulness of the world. The need for the Cross remained. But his coming to earth was a resounding "nevertheless"—God's pronouncement that the world, the flesh, and the devil do not have the last word. There is a word greater than all our sin—a word that will ultimately bring an end to every form of pain and even death itself. When we pray "nevertheless" prayers, we do not ignore reality or minimize anyone's condition. Instead, we declare that we will not be defined by evil but by God.

I believe there are situations that will not change on this earth. There are depths of sickness and suffering that will not be eliminated, even by devout intercession. Even when miracles occur, the larger reality remains. I know people who were snatched from death's door but later died. I've known people delivered from one problem only to have an even worse one come to them later. We live in a fallen world; even the advent of Christ could not change that fact. What he changed was the belief that the devil has the final say. So we pray, "nevertheless."

I hope your theology of prayer includes heaven. Properly viewed, heaven is not an escape from reality. Heaven is much more significant than that. It is the place where all the evil that has held this cosmos captive will be once and for all removed. This belief is not naïveté—a "pie in the sky in the sweet by and by" faith—but rather a long, hard look at reality, with the conclusion that for life to be as God originally intended, there must be a place where sickness and suffering do not prevail. Paul was correct: if all we have to hope for is that everything will eventually turn out all right here on earth, "we are of all people most to be pitied" (1 Cor. 15:19).

I write this as one who has suffered little in comparison to many others. But I have visited places of immense and unrelenting suffering. I have known people who have endured unimaginable pain. Each day I read, hear, and watch news reports that tell me that in many parts of the world, things are not getting better. This is reality, but it is not the ultimate truth. The defining truth is this: everyone caught up in every conceivable form of evil has the possibility of an eternity that differs radically from current circumstances. Destruction, disease, deformity, and destitution do not have the last word. God has the last word. "Nevertheless" prayer affirms that truth.

Second, *"nevertheless" prayer enables us to embrace revelation.* I had been a Christian for a while before I realized that the message for us is not that all suffering will be eliminated, but that grace is given to enable us to cope with it. For reasons we will never completely understand, God does not eliminate suffering; but God comes to us in suffering. I came to this view by reading several significant Bible stories through a new lens.

I read about Adam and Eve in Genesis 3. When they sinned, God's original intentions for creation became radically altered. The Bible has hardly begun before all of God's purposes get changed. The blessings of Edenic existence become the curses resulting from our parents' primal sin. But then we see something amazing: God walks in the Garden, this time without Adam and Eve. They are hiding. But God walks, looking for them. And when he finds them, he provides clothing to cover their nakedness. In the first story of scripture, God writes a "nevertheless" into the picture. Sin will remain, but it will not ultimately reign. God stays committed to the human family and provides a way of redemption in a situation that just a little while before didn't need it. This revelation, given at the very beginning of the biblical narrative, enables us to read the rest of the Bible in a completely different way.

One evening as we were putting our children to bed, our daughter, Katrina (about two years old at the time), asked, "Daddy, if Adam and Eve sinned so much, why didn't God just crumple up the world and start all over?" We had read about Adam and Eve that night during our devotional time, and she was confused. In her mind, she saw God dealing with Adam and Eve's sin just as she would handle a mistake made while drawing a picture. When she messed up, she crumpled the paper, took out a new sheet, and started over. Why didn't God do the same? Because God could not destroy a creation that had eternal value—even after the Fall. The only option for God was redemption. Likewise, God will not allow the immense suffering of this world to have the final word. Evil does not define God's continuing creation; righteousness does. In Christ, God has provided a way through and a way out when life doesn't make sense. That's the final word, and it occurs right at the front of the Bible.

The second story I viewed through a new lens is God's call to Moses, recorded in Exodus 3. When Moses stands before the burning bush, God says, "I have observed the misery of my people . . . and I have come down to deliver them" (vv. 7-8). As in Eden, God is walking on the earth again, to deliver the children of Israel from the oppression of their Egyptian taskmasters. This time God will use a human agent (Moses) to set the people free. Moses is God's "nevertheless" spoken in the midst of slavery and misery.

The third story emerged from my reading of the Twenty-third Psalm. A familiar phrase took on new meaning: "Yea, though I walk through the valley of the shadow of death, I will fear no evil; for thou art with me; thy rod and thy staff they comfort me" (v. 4, KJV). Clearly the psalmist was not allowed to bypass that valley but was called to walk *through* it—yet not alone. Another was with him, and that companion was God's "nevertheless" given when life is as dark as it gets.

I could continue, for scripture contains many other stories where God reveals a "nevertheless." You will see them for yourself if you have not done so already. If the reality is that suffering is part of the human story, then the revelation is that we never have to face that suffering alone. God comes to us in one way or another. We are given a companion—sometimes through the Holy Spirit, sometimes through other people, and sometimes through both—a companionship that becomes a graced strength giving us power to endure. When this vision became imbedded in me, it changed how I pray.

Finally, *"nevertheless" prayer leads us to make a response.* For me, the response is best captured in what Brennan Manning often calls "ruthless trust." Isn't that what the word *nevertheless* means? Isn't this what Maltbie Babcock intended when he wrote, "that though the wrong seems oft so strong, God is the ruler yet"?[1] When we can accept the reality of life and embrace the revelation of God in the midst of it, our praying becomes a powerful response enabling us to face what comes our way with profound trust. I see such trust in these powerful words of Saint Paul:

> I am convinced that neither death, nor life, nor angels, nor rulers, nor things present, nor things to come, nor powers, nor height, nor depth, nor anything else in all creation, will be able to separate us from the love of God in Christ Jesus our Lord. (Romans 8:38-39)

I have come to believe that these verses, more than any other passage in the Bible, are foundational for a Christian theology of prayer.

Paul was no superman, and he certainly did not develop his theology of prayer while lying on a bed of ease. He responded to the reality of life around him and the condition of his soul within him. On more than one occasion life could have done him in—except for one thing: he was convinced that God had the last word. Paul had no hope in himself, but he had enormous hope in God. When he prayed, he was not engaging in psychological self-talk; he was communicating in spiritual "God talk."

It is precisely here that I want to live and pray. I want to stand on the bedrock conviction that God has the last word. Sometimes God speaks that word in this world, and we call it answered prayer, which comes in the forms of insights, deliverances, strengthenings, and miracles.

At other times, God speaks that word by transitioning us from this world into the next through the experience of death. Either way, God has put a "nevertheless" into the picture that enables us to say:

> The light shines in the darkness, and the darkness did not overcome it. (John 1:5)

Continue to pray—nevertheless!

PART TWO

EXPRESSIONS

Pray at all times
and on every occasion
in the power of the Holy Spirit.

—EPHESIANS 6:18, NLT

Our prayer life will become restful
when it really dawns upon us that
we have done all we are supposed to do
when we have spoken to [God] about it.
From that moment we have left it
with [God]. It is [God's] responsibility.

—O. HALLESBY

PRELUDE
TO PART TWO

Prayer is God's 24/7 gift to us. We can pray anytime, anywhere, and about anything. As I tried to show in Part One, our prayers express our deepest beliefs about God, ourselves, the church, and so forth. In working with people over the years, I've discovered that in certain life situations prayer becomes more of a struggle—particularly when we go through extended periods of spiritual dryness or face a crisis we didn't see coming. Beyond those two significant experiences, there are also questions about the value of intercessory prayer and how we are to go about praying for ourselves.

I have selected these four areas as the focal points for Part Two. I'm confident that even as you read this section of the book, you are addressing at least one of these areas in your life right now. I hope you will see that what I've written in Part One helps to shape our praying under these circumstances. I haven't pulled any punches in this section of the book. The people I've described are real and their situations significant. I did not gloss over their struggles or minimize their pain. But each of them exemplifies how we can keep praying when life doesn't make sense.

CHAPTER 5

PRAYING WHEN YOU'RE DRY

When the train goes through a tunnel and the world becomes dark, do you jump out? Of course not. You sit still and trust the engineer to get you through.

—CORRIE TEN BOOM

Charles asked to see me after the evening worship service. When he entered my office, I could tell from the look on his face that this would not be a casual conversation. He closed the door behind him and wasted no time getting to the point: "For the past eighteen months, I have felt like God is moving farther and farther away. I am pretty much just going through the motions of my faith. My soul feels as dry as a desert."

The dryness he was feeling was made all the worse because, as Charles went on to tell me, he had experienced God in a dramatic way several years before. He had even thought God might be calling him to be an ordained minister. The first ten years or so of his Christian life had been what he expected, as he seriously sought to live out his discipleship through his church membership, his marriage and family life, and his vocation. But despite all that, he revealed a downward spiral of spiritual erosion. And by the time he came to talk to me, he was the most discouraged he had ever been in his Christian life.

Charles was the first person to be that honest with me about his spiritual condition. I must confess that as a young pastor, I was surprised and somewhat taken back by his remarks. One of the leaders in our congregation, Charles was one of my best supporters. We were good friends, and I had no idea that he felt so depleted. Charles had continued to show up for worship, Wednesday evening fellowship, administrative meetings, and pretty much anything else he needed to do to be helpful. But inside it was another story. And he wanted me to know that he would not be participating in a prayer study our church had launched that evening. He just didn't have it in him to try to pray to a God who was becoming more and more distant to him.

I don't remember saying anything that helped Charles in that moment. I'm sure I expressed some surprise and sadness, and I hope I told him it was okay not to be involved in the prayer emphasis. But what I remember mostly is that we talked a little longer, I said a short prayer, and he left as quickly as he had come. I still remember my feelings as I stood alone in my study, gathered my belongings, and walked the short distance to the parsonage, in the dark.

Part of what bothered me about the whole incident is that some of what Charles had told me was part of my own experience. At that time, I had never had an extended period of spiritual dryness, but I surely knew what it was to feel as if God was moving closer at times and farther away at others. I shared Charles's confusion about that, but, like him, I realized that the church rarely speaks about this condition. And even though I was somewhat dumbfounded by my conversation with Charles that evening, I am dumbfounded no longer. Since that evening, Charles has been joined by many others who felt safe enough to share their stories with me, and I've had the opportunity to share mine with them. Spiritual dryness is a condition that makes prayer feel as though we're talking in the dark.

I've come to believe that spiritual dryness is the most often felt and least often discussed experience in the Christian life. The church does not usually provide places where we can be that honest, and even when it does, we're not sure how to put our struggle into words, nor do we feel confident that people will hear what we are trying to say. When we are in positions of leadership, that kind of confession proves even more difficult. So, we come to church and go through all the motions that communicate the message, "I'm in as good a shape as any of the rest of you"—even when we're not. When we're having a particularly down time, we may even ask sarcastically, "How can these people around me be so happy when I feel so sad?" The gap between appearance and reality feels like a wide gulf and a heavy weight.

The question arises, How do we continue to pray when it seems that God has moved away and left no forwarding address? How do we pray when the sense of God's silence and absence is almost overwhelming? These questions are very personal, and each of us experiences them differently. I can only tell you how I have dealt with them as I've struggled with extended periods of spiritual dryness.

When I began to pay attention to spiritual dryness, I met Asaph, to whom Psalm 77 is attributed. He was most likely a Levite who served as a worship leader during the reigns of

David and Solomon. What struck me was the fact that he became spiritually dry in the midst of leading Israel's praise and worship. He went dry in the Temple! Though devoted, gifted, and esteemed, Asaph experienced the sense of God's absence in his life. Psalm 77 is his recounting of that experience. If you have a Bible at hand, open it to that passage. You will be able to read the rest of this chapter much more meaningfully.

Without ever intending to, and perhaps without ever expecting to, Asaph is leading the choir but not hearing the music. We can only imagine how he must have felt about inviting worshipers to draw near to God, even as he felt that he was slipping away. Psalm 77 shows us some of the anguish he felt and the questions he raised. But remember, that psalm is a prayer. When Asaph was dry, he prayed—right in the middle of it all, he talked with God. And perhaps the reason he eventually composed Psalm 77 was because he discovered he was not the only one feeling that way. This was a prayer for a community to pray, not just individuals. As the psalm clearly shows, Asaph did not mince words. He did not hide his questions or hold back his emotions. Asaph is the patron saint for all of us who become spiritually dry and have to decide how (or if) we are going to pray in that condition. He comes to us in our dryness and says, "Don't stop praying, but pray like this."

First, Asaph *reminds us to pray with the realization that spiritual dryness is normal.* I wish I had met him, or someone like him, sooner. I mistakenly believed dryness was a sign of drifting or defection. I had even read material that gave this counsel: "When you become dry, ask God to show you what sins you've committed." Dryness was viewed as the warning light on the dashboard of my car, telling me to pull over and check the engine because something was wrong. No one ever advised me to think of dryness in any other way. Looking back on that perspective, I have two responses.

The first is that dryness can indeed be an indicator of sin. At times in my spiritual life I ask, "God, is this dry spell due to some sin?" and God responds, "I'm glad you asked; we need to talk." There is no doubt that unconfessed sin can damage our prayer lives, because it damages our relationships with God. So when I experience spiritual dryness, I never exclude the possibility that sin could be the cause.

> THERE IS NO DOUBT THAT UNCONFESSED SIN CAN DAMAGE OUR PRAYER LIVES, BECAUSE IT DAMAGES OUR RELATIONSHIPS WITH GOD.

But my second response, thanks to Asaph, is this: sin is not the only cause of dryness. Psalm 77 contains no evidence that Asaph had sinned. Once I saw that, I met many other bona fide saints whose dryness I had never paid attention to. Teresa of Ávila endured the longest period of dryness I've ever heard of: twenty years! George Fox, founder of the Quakers, wrote in his journal about a five-year period when access to heaven seemed closed to him. Less than a year after John Wesley's heart-warming experience at Aldersgate, he wrote in his journal that he was certain he was not a Christian and wondered whether he had ever been one. I continue to learn of men and women, ancient and modern, whose spiritual journeys took them into the wilderness. Rather than discouraging me, their testimonies give me hope. I realize I am not alone in my experience of dryness. Like them, I realize I can continue to pray.

One of my life's blessings has been the opportunity to study the devotional life of John Wesley in great detail. In doing so, I read extensively from his diaries. I discovered he used symbols in his diary to evaluate his spiritual condition. For example, when he prayed, he simply wrote the letter *p*. He indicated how meaningful his prayers were by drawing a short line above, through, or below the *p*. If his prayers were "warm and effectual," he put the line above the letter. If his prayers were mediocre, he drew the line through the letter. And if his prayers were "cold and indifferent," he drew the line below the letter.

It soon became clear in reading Wesley's diaries that there were many days, and sometimes several days in a row, when the line was below the letter—meaning his prayers were "cold and indifferent." Or to say it another way, he could not tell if his prayers were making any difference whatsoever. But here's the significant fact: even when that was the case, he did not stop praying. There might be many times when the line was below the letter, but *p* did not disappear from his diary. It was John Wesley's "nevertheless" kind of praying.

It is difficult for me to overstate the importance of persistence. One of the serious problems with spiritual dryness is that it makes us feel like not praying. After all, we say to ourselves, what difference does it make? We cannot tell that anything is going on inside our hearts, and if God is hearing our prayers, we can't tell that either. So we are inclined to quit. But Wesley's witness—and the witness of so many others—is that to stop praying is a big mistake. It is a mistake because it makes sensibility the measure rather than faith. And it takes away the sacred place where God is most likely to come back to us. If God has been real to us in prayer, it will probably be in prayer that God will become real to us again. Therefore, to give up praying cuts us off from the very medium where renewal will come. Asaph seems to have known that, for he continued to pray in the midst of his dryness.

Second, *Asaph teaches us to pray honestly when we are spiritually dry*. His prayer was not nice and neat but real, and God always honors authenticity. Asaph did not hide his feelings, questions, or fears. Similarly, when we are dry, we do not help our cause if we "fake it to make it." We do not solve our problem by keeping prayer safe and clean—and superficial. Asaph takes us into the depths of his dryness, and rather than finding a God who is offended by honesty, he finds One who can handle whatever we have to say. As you may recall, this is part of what I tried to say in chapter 1. But it bears reemphasizing in our examination of spiritual dryness. Prolonged periods of God's seeming absence create wear and tear on our souls. We might as well admit it when we feel God's absence, and we can include that admission in our prayers.

WE DO NOT SOLVE OUR PROBLEM BY KEEPING PRAYER SAFE AND CLEAN—AND SUPERFICIAL.

Years ago, I heard the testimony of a man who prayed this way: "God, if you exist—and I am not sure you do—please hear this prayer. And if you do hear this prayer—and I am not sure you will—please answer it." The man went on to say that God did hear and answer. His was a tentative prayer experiment, to be sure, but it was enough to move him past his doubts into a deepening journey of prayer. Of course, we can as easily imagine that the man's experiment might not have worked. Had that been the case, I probably would not include his story in this book. But I think you can see that this man's prayer did not differ greatly from the way Asaph prayed in Psalm 77. The point is simply this: we are able, even invited, to pray to God as honestly as we know how. If you don't believe that, then how do you explain Jesus' cry from the cross, "My God, my God, why have you forsaken me?"

Do you believe you can be that honest in prayer? As honest as Asaph, as honest as the man whose story I just shared, as honest as Jesus? If this kind of praying is new to you or feels like a stretch, take some time to read through the book of Psalms. If you have a study Bible that has a list of the prayers of the Bible, read those passages too. I guarantee that you will emerge from that reading with a new view of prayer. You will come to see that not only can God handle honesty, but God desires it. Honesty gives God room to work. When we are superficial and artificial in our praying, it's more difficult for God to respond to us as we really are. Asaph's honesty meant he was open to God from top to bottom. God can always deal with us when we are that open.

YOU WILL COME TO SEE THAT NOT ONLY CAN GOD HANDLE HONESTY, BUT GOD DESIRES IT.

Third, *Asaph's prayer seeks to know the cause of his dryness*. His questions in verses 7-9 indicate that he is probing himself and God for any light that can be shed on his dilemma. Realizing that in this case, sin is not the cause of his dryness, he looks for other reasons. This approach only stands to reason. The more we are able to understand the cause of our dryness, the more fully we can cooperate with God in dealing with it.

I learned this in my most severe bout with spiritual dryness. It came in the mid-1980s while I was teaching courses on prayer at Asbury Theological Seminary. I was even writing a devotional commentary on the book of Acts. But little by little, God seemed to fade away—and stay away for seven months. I kept at my work and never stopped believing that what I was teaching and writing was true. The frustration was that I was offering a view of God to others that was not being confirmed in my day-to-day life. Like Asaph, I had no unconfessed sin. In fact, I came close several times to confessing sins I'd never committed, just in case that would help! I was growing more and more discouraged and desperate.

One day, while working on the book at home, I stopped to take a break. I went to the kitchen, opened the refrigerator, and poured myself a glass of iced tea. I went back to my study to drink the tea—and God came back. Just as surely as I had sensed God's absence, now I sensed God's presence. It happened that quickly and definitely. I had done nothing to make it happen, and I had no anticipation that it would happen. But it did.

When God's presence returned, God came speaking. "Do you know what your problem has been?"

I have to tell you, that question upset me. I responded tersely, "Of course I don't know what my problem is! If I knew that, I would have done something about it a long time ago . . . Amen."

The inner voice continued, "Would you like to know what your problem is?"

Ah, that was another question, and I said with a different emotion, "Yes, Lord, I would like to know."

And I heard deep in my being: "Steve, your problem is that you have been *working* for me, but you haven't been *walking* with me. You need to realize that I do not have employees in my kingdom. I have only beloved sons and daughters."

That day I learned that my perceived status with God influences my sense of relationship with God. I learned that nothing can take the place of knowing I am a beloved child of God. I found the cause of my dryness: substituting a professional relationship with God for a personal one. Now, more than twenty years later, knowing that cause has saved me from similar pitfalls. When I am tempted to put other things in place of my personal walk with God, I quickly feel a check in my spirit, and I do whatever it takes to keep my relationship rooted in love, not performance.

In my years of working with all sorts of people, I have discovered other reasons for prolonged periods of spiritual dryness. I do not have the luxury of writing about each of them extensively in this chapter. But perhaps mentioning them will be of some help to you. Maybe one of these causes will be the very one you need to discover in order to regain vitality in your prayer life. One of the main causes is what I call "affective breakdown." This simply means that we cannot expect to maintain forever an even emotional life with God, any more so than we do with other people. We accept as normal the fact that emotions fluctuate, so we should not be surprised when our emotions rise and fall in our relationship with God.

Another cause is physiological. A change in hormones or metabolism can create a sense of God's absence. Disease can also drain us of spiritual vitality. Depression can alter the chemical balances in our brains and create the sense that God has departed. Improper sleep patterns, a poor diet, and insufficient exercise can contribute as well. We are a culture burning the candle at both ends, treating our bodies in ways they were never designed to tolerate. We pay a high price for this lack of self-care, including a depletion in our spiritual lives.

Spiritual underfeeding can also create dryness. We cannot expect to maintain an authentic relationship with God when we give God the leftovers of our lives. We cannot pretend to be overflowing in our relationship with God when we are half-full in our devotion. "Churchianity" is no substitute for Christianity. Spiritual overfeeding will also make us dry. Religion can become an obsession. But God is the God of life, not just of spirituality. Some people do not need a deeper life; they need a broader one.

Imitating others will also bring on dryness. God creates individuals, not clones. We can learn from others, but we must not seek to become them. Still another cause is change. When we move from one stage of life to another or from one place to another, we can sometimes expect to feel a decline in our spiritual vitality. And finally, we will become dry if we do not put into practice what we are discovering. It will do us no good to have a great devotional time on the subject of patience and then go out of our prayer closet to yell at the kids and kick the dog. There must be congruence between the interior and the exterior.

I am sure there are more causes of spiritual dryness than I have noted in this chapter, and I realize that I have only briefly dealt with the ones I selected. I may have failed to mention the reason you've felt spiritually bereft. But I hope these examples are enough to help you see that knowing the cause gives you a starting place for working with God to restore authenticity to your prayer life. Remember, you will not always be able to know the cause. But like Asaph, you can turn your questions into prayers and endure.

Fourth, *Asaph used memory to hold him secure when his present experience of God was faltering*. He remembered the deeds of the Lord and the miracles of God from long ago. Even though his current experience of God had been taken away, nothing could change the fact that he had known God's goodness and mercy in the past. Asaph could lose the sense of God's presence only because he had once had it. Any grace experienced is grace available. The fact that we do not perceive the "now" of God does not mean all we have is the "never" of God.

I knew of a pastor in Texas who kept a row of black notebooks on his bookshelves, just behind his office chair. When a friend of mine asked him what the notebooks were, the pastor replied, "They are my prayer journals." Then he quickly added, "When I feel discouraged in my prayer life, all I have to do is swivel around and look at those notebooks. I remember that God has answered my prayers." I do not know what you will use to rouse your memory, but I can tell you that being able to remember rich times with God in prayer is a precious gift when you go through periods of dryness. When you cannot pray your todays or your tomorrows, pray your yesterdays.

Finally, *Asaph teaches us that dryness does not last forever*. It is not a terminal disease. From verse 13 to the end of Psalm 77, Asaph reveals a gradual return of the vitality he had lost. Amazingly, his prayer moved from profound questions about God to his exclamation, "What god is so great as our God?" Likewise, we may not know when or how our experience of God will change, but we do know that the rivers of living water will flow again. A day will come when the rain of God's Spirit will water our parched souls. It is against that backdrop that we pray when we are dry.

CHAPTER 6

PRAYING WHEN LIFE SUDDENLY CHANGES

[God] did not say: You will not be troubled,
you will not be tempted, you will not be distressed.
But [God] said: You will not be overcome.

—JULIAN OF NORWICH

Joy called to tell me her cancer had returned. She had been disease free for several years, but now the cancer was back with a vengeance. I had been Joy's pastor for a year, and I still remembered when she had first told me she was "cancer free." The joy in her voice and her name were one. But today it was different. Life had suddenly changed. Jeannie and I wept with her and her husband, Jim, as we dealt with this devastating news. In one visit to the doctor, all of Joy's health and hope were dashed by a new report. She was admitted to the hospital for what turned out to be her final battle with the disease.

Jeannie's and my visits with Joy in those final months created precious memories that we carry with us to this day. But the greatest gift Joy gave us—and many others—was showing us how to live as a person of prayer when life suddenly changes. She taught us that lesson right up to the last minute we saw her. Jim and Joy decided to make one last-ditch effort to cure the cancer at M. D. Anderson Cancer Center in Houston, Texas. Getting her there required a trip by air ambulance. The morning for her departure arrived quickly. Jeannie and I drove to our little airport and parked within feet of the airplane. Joy had just arrived from the hospital and lay on the stretcher, waiting to be placed on the plane. We moved toward her, and she reached out her hand to me. We both knew it would probably be the last time we would hold hands.

Time froze. I knew I needed to say something, but I had used up all my words on previous visits. In the preceding weeks we had prayed, anointed Joy with oil, and discussed nearly every part of her life. The work had been done. The decks had been cleared. Joy was at peace with God. Yet as we joined hands on the tarmac, something begged to be said. I looked at Joy, and she looked at me with her steel-blue eyes. I can still see her face in my mind's eye. All I could muster through my own tear-filled eyes and broken voice was this: "Joy, it's going to be okay." And that's when it happened. From a depth of reality only Joy was experiencing, she spoke back to me: "Steve, it *is* okay." We all knew what she meant.

On the day of her funeral, it was still okay. Joy had taken some of us farther and deeper than we had ever gone before. Heaven and earth met on that tarmac, in the funeral home, and at the cemetery. The depth of grace bestowed through her experience revealed how pervasively God can work. Grace was flowing inside Joy even before she called to tell me her cancer was back. And it continued to flow, even when her pain was worse than the medications could control. Grace was offered when we said prayers aloud and when we prayed silently. Joy taught us how to pray in the face of sudden need—in the face of a need that does not get better.

First, *Joy taught us that we pray in relation to stored-up resources.* Life can change quickly. Joy woke up one morning feeling fine, but her doctor's appointment revealed another story. She could not have "manufactured" enough grace to cope with the news, but she was able to draw from the grace in which she was already living to face it. When life suddenly changes, the best thing we have going for us is a long-standing relationship with God. We do not "get grace" so much as we live in grace over the long haul. Joy's deep faith afforded a dispensation of grace when her health changed without warning.

Deep wells provide good water. Joy did not have to muster up grace when she heard the bad news; rather, she drew from the well of grace that had already been dug in her relationship with God. When Joy looked at me and said, "Steve, it *is* okay," she was speaking from a place that years of prayer and devotion had constructed for her. If I could offer you one piece of advice about praying when life suddenly changes, I would say, "Don't wait for the change to occur. If you haven't already done so, begin now to dig the well that leads to God's living water, so that when your change happens, you can draw from resources that are already present."

Since my experience with Joy, I have seen something in the life of Jesus that changed my view of grace and its ability to carry us through tough times. For a while Jesus experienced great success and popularity. But as with any high moment, it was also a time of pressure and responsibility. It was also a time when Jesus' own sense of achievement and sense of mission could easily have caused him to say, "My ministry is going exactly the way I had hoped. I'll get back to prayer when things calm down." But rather than taking this approach, Jesus withdrew to deserted places so he could pray.

That's the secret of Jesus' endurance when the tide turned against him. He did not squander the good days or believe that he had created them in his own strength. Instead, he knew the source of his power, and he drew from it day after day. God's reservoir of grace sustained him when things were going well, and because he kept going to that reservoir to drink, grace was available when receptivity turned into opposition and shouts of affirmation changed into calls for his crucifixion. Jesus did not use prayer like a rip cord on a parachute; rather, he practiced it regularly for spiritual nourishment. Joy used prayer the same way when life suddenly changed for her. When life suddenly changes, how do we pray? We pray as we have been praying for a long time.

* JESUS DID NOT USE PRAYER LIKE A RIP CORD ON A PARACHUTE; RATHER, HE PRACTICED IT REGULARLY FOR SPIRITUAL NOURISHMENT.

Second, *Joy welcomed fresh waves of grace into the new reality of her life.* She was not drinking stale water or praying old prayers. She found current nourishment in the presence of the risen Christ. Often when I visited her, she began the time by saying, "Let me tell you what's been going on since you were here last." Sometimes it was something connected with her treatment in the hospital. Sometimes it was an experience given through a telephone call, card, or visit. She even received fresh insights from her dreams. She was living out the reality of the Twenty-third Psalm, "Yea, though I walk through the valley of the shadow of death, I will fear no evil: for thou art with me." And the Good Shepherd was there.

Interestingly, she reached a point where she didn't feel the need to be prayed for every time someone else came to see her. I remember the first time it happened with me. In my customary pastoral approach, I said, "Joy, before I go, I want to pray for you." Without skipping a beat she said, "No, let's just keep talking a little while longer. You have prayed for me enough for now." She was not minimizing prayer; she was trying to tell me that the glory of God was filling her room and her life in ways far beyond the minutes I might spend with her in prayer. She was telling me that all the necessary words had been spoken. It was enough. I honored her request, and we kept talking a little while longer. But as we did, I remember a sense of God's presence surrounding us. God was continuing to give her the grace she needed when she needed it. It was enough.

There is a deep mystery of the risen Christ that does not require words. In fact, words sometimes get in the way. God does not give or withhold ministry based on whether or not we speak. For those of us who speak often or speak professionally, this is a very important lesson to learn. And for those of us who suffer, it is also important to know that God will come to us in grace-filled silence, speaking a word that only the soul can hear. Joy heard that Voice, and other people did not have to be speaking in order for her to feel cared for by God.

For many years, Jeannie and I have been inspired by the life and ministry of Amy Carmichael. After decades of faithful missionary ministry in India, Amy injured herself one night when she fell into a hole. Her accident opened the way for debilitating rheumatoid arthritis to ravage her body. For much of the rest of her life, she was confined to her bed. At first, she felt that her ministry was over. But her confinement became a means to hear God speaking to her in deeper ways than ever before. Some of her most inspiring writings come from this period in her life. One of the most important lessons she learned and shared was that access to God's presence does not require a lot of effort—what she called "pushing." The deeper secret, she found, was receptivity. This disposition opens a person to God's ministry through the Spirit without having to know how it will work or when it will come.

Joy lived this reality as her cancer progressed. Far from rejecting the prayers of the church, she found that they stood alongside an unceasing access to the presence of God. Every moment was a "God moment," not just the moments devoted specifically to prayer or to religious conversation. She had moved to another place in the great house of God—a place where simply being with God was enough. Such a place did not guarantee that each day would be a good day, but it did transform every day into a God day. Fresh waves of grace rolled into Joy's life, keeping her experience with God current and real.

When I reflect on the importance of God's fresh appearances, I think of Dr. William Barclay. Dr. Barclay's commentaries have inspired several generations of Christians. But not everyone knows of a tragedy that befell him and his wife. I heard the story one day during one of Dr. Barclay's radio broadcasts. A caller asked him if he believed Jesus calmed the storm on the sea of Galilee. In a somewhat unusual response, Dr. Barclay said, "Before I answer that question, let me tell you something even more important."

He told of his daughter, who had fallen in love with a marvelous young man. The young man proposed to her; she accepted, and they set the wedding date. The Barclays pulled out all the stops to make their daughter's wedding a grand occasion. They planned a wonderful dinner beside a lake after the rehearsal. When the time came for the dinner, the daughter and her fiancé decided that rather than traveling to the restaurant by car, they would take a romantic rowboat ride across the lake. So everyone in the wedding party set out for the dinner.

But Dr. Barclay's daughter and her fiancé never arrived. A storm churned the waters of the lake, capsizing the little boat. The young couple drowned. And instead of a wedding, Dr. Barclay and his wife attended the funeral of their daughter. When he finished telling that story on the radio, he added, "My dear caller, the most important question is not whether Jesus calmed the storm on the sea two thousand years ago; the most important question is whether or not he can calm the storms in our lives today. And I am here to tell you that he can."

Joy was not living on a rumor from the past that God could comfort the afflicted. She was experiencing up-to-the-minute confirmation that God still comforts people today.

Third, *Joy's understanding of God's comfort enabled her to find blessings in things that happened to her along the way.* Cancer was not Joy's friend, but the disease brought her many visits and numerous cards, flowers, and phone calls. She cherished them all. And I am sure she and Jim shared treasured moments as husband and wife. Some of my memorable moments with Joy occurred when we talked about heaven. If Joy had not been heading there, I doubt she would have talked about it the way she did. She had questions, and she knew that some of them did not have answers in this life. Nevertheless, it was interesting to engage in some sanctified speculation about eternal life. As she moved closer to heaven, Joy's comments seemed to come more "from" heaven than be "about" heaven. It was as if a window had opened in her hospital room—a window enabling her to see her situation differently, in relation to a new reality. I learned more about heaven in those days than I ever did in a seminary classroom.

Jeannie and I have shared the same experience with other people, including parents and friends. In particular, Jeannie's dad taught us all how to face death with courage and faith. When doctors determined that he needed a radical amputation but the amputation would not ultimately prevent his death, Jim decided to forego the operation and go on to heaven. The final ten days of his life were a blessing to us all, but they were not easy. Our hearts were sad, but every member of the family drew strength from Jim's courage.

Something happens when life changes suddenly. Life looks different than it used to. Values change; conversations change; perspectives shift. We use our time differently. People become much more precious to us than possessions. Ordinary moments become charged with significance and with the energy of eternity. Prayer weaves its way into this tapestry, creating moments of reflection and gratitude. Prayer becomes a spiritual Velcro to which other things stick. What seems to be loss on one level gets transformed into gain on another level. Prayer enables us to see every moment as a gift and as an occasion to cherish.

Finally, and perhaps most importantly, *prayer takes us to the place where we are healed of the need to be healed.* Joy reached that point. She never ceased to cooperate with the best wisdom of her doctors, including that last-ditch trip to Houston for an experimental treatment. But she no longer *had* to get well. To have prayed for her healing, once she came to this new place, would have been to steal from her an even deeper experience of

God's presence and grace. Her suffering was not the end of the story, and as she entered more fully into an experience she could not change, she wanted us to see with her "the other side" that was becoming more real to her than her deteriorating condition. We stopped praying that Joy would not die, and we began to pray instead what Christians for centuries have prayed—for her to experience a *blessed* death. Joy was able to let go of our hands because she was in God's hands. Once we realized that, we did not try to reestablish our grip on her life.

PRAYER ENABLES US TO SEE EVERY MOMENT AS A GIFT AND AS AN OCCASION TO CHERISH.

Today we greatly need to regain the theology of "holy dying." When someone's life ends, it is not *the* end. We live in a world where medical technology can preserve life beyond reasonable limits. Hope can get lost whenever we feel we must get well or have our problems solved. Prayer can deteriorate into a spiritual bargaining process rather than being a means to see our present reality from an eternal perspective.

But when viewed as Joy came to view it, prayer can lead us to what may be our deepest life experience: the healing of the need to be healed. We do not have to have health restored in order to have hope. We do not have to cling desperately to life in this world when we see life in relationship to the world to come. This life is not all there is. More awaits us, and prayer makes it possible for us to catch a glimpse of eternal life. Prayer becomes a means of grace that enables us to loosen our hold on time so that we can put our hands on eternity.

All of that was taking place on the tarmac when Joy spoke her last words to me: "Steve, it *is* okay." And since then, Jeannie and I have been privileged to walk with others to the same place—the place where, deep in the love of God, it is okay. Even when we talk in the dark and walk on a path we cannot see, we know we are not alone, and we know the path is there. It is okay.

CHAPTER 7

PRAYING FOR OTHERS

Intercession means that we rouse ourselves up to get the mind of Christ about the one for whom we pray.

—OSWALD CHAMBERS

Fred raised his hand and asked the question everyone wonders about: "Does praying for others really make a difference?" He followed immediately with the accompanying question: "And even if it does, how could you ever know?"

When we think of prayer as talking in the dark, there's no darker place than intercessory prayer. The darkness is not merely philosophical or inquisitive; it almost always relates to real-life experience. We know that some people for whom we pray are healed, and others are not. We've known of families celebrating the news that a loved one would soon come home from the battlefield, only to learn later that the soldier was killed just before the scheduled return. In raising his questions, Fred was no skeptic; he was merely asking what has the right to be asked. It's normal to inquire about matters we want to understand, and it is not unusual to raise questions about situations that don't have simple answers or fit predictable patterns.

We are simply joining with the rest of the human family when we ask, "What difference does praying for others make?"

For me, the issue is not *whether* to ask questions but rather to learn *how* to ask them. The motive behind the question is significant. To be honest, I have little patience with cynics when it comes to prayer questions. I realize that life can make us bitter, but I've never seen anyone get better or stronger by becoming cynical. I have lost most of my interest in playing "mental chess" with people who intend nothing more than to stir up controversy. I have not written this chapter for people like that. I have written it for people who come to intercessory prayer with no reservations or hidden agendas but the desire to learn to pray for others more effectively and meaningfully. What, then, do we discover when we question intercessory prayer in that way?

First, we find mystery. And for some of us, that's the hardest part. After all, we don't ask questions unless we expect to get answers. But we simply will not find an answer to every question about intercession. We must prepare ourselves for that reality. How do we make that preparation? I believe we do it the same way we do with a lot of other things in life: we press on. I wish prayer were the only thing I don't understand, but it isn't. When I think about it, I live with mystery every day of my life. I could make a list of things I don't understand that would continue for pages. Some of the mysteries are insignificant and routine; others are substantial and formidable.

For me, this means that the real issue with intercessory prayer is not that it is a mystery. I would worry about that if it were the only mystery I have to face, but it isn't. On the contrary, I have learned to live quite naturally with all sorts of mysteries. We operate machinery; use technology; travel by land, air, and sea; do business; and form relationships without understanding how everything works. But we press on. So, with respect to intercessory prayer, one of our first challenges is to treat it as we do almost every other mystery—that is, to see it as a mixture of the known and the unknown.

I do not mean to minimize anyone's experience with intercession by taking this approach. I have sat with people whose lives were shattered by experiences that did not turn out the way they had hoped—and prayed. Mystery brings deep pain sometimes. I would never want to put anything in this chapter that would ignore that reality. But I must tell you that intercessory prayer was saved for me when I realized that I did not have to understand it in order to practice it. I am an analytical person. As long as I can remember, I have always wanted to know the "why" and "how" of things. I naturally carried this inclination with me into the study of theology in general and prayer in particular.

When I hit the wall of mystery, I had a decision to make. I could turn around and say, "Well, that's it for me. I can't live with or practice what I don't understand." Or I could face the wall, build a ladder, and see as much on the other side as possible. I chose the second option. Ironically, mystery has not diminished my faith; instead, it has increased it. Life on the other side of mystery is larger and more real because I see that life is bigger, more complex, and infinitely more interesting than anything I can conceive. In fact, I had to come to the place where I could acknowledge that faith I can understand is actually faith in myself, not in God. One of the prerequisites for intercession is an "unknowing" that takes me out of the center of things and allows God to dwell there.

This immediately saves us from perhaps the worst mistake we can make about intercessory prayer—thinking our prayer was not answered because we didn't have "enough faith," didn't pray often enough, or didn't get enough people to pray along with us. I have met people who were absolutely tormented by notions like these. But these ideas simply are not true, and to believe such lies only gives the evil one room to fill us with guilt, doubt, and remorse.

But there is a great challenge in this approach. When you take yourself out of the center (that is, out of the place of understanding) and put God there, it makes all the difference what kind of God you put there. If you're not careful, you can re-create the "God problem" I tried to address in chapter 1. Without reviewing that, let me simply say that it is very important to trust the God who is, in fact, trustworthy. We must put our theology and practice of intercessory prayer on the foundation of revelation. Since I do not know you or your situation, I can only exhort you to take whatever time you need to connect yourself to the God who loves you and cares about you. This will not answer every question you have about intercessory prayer, but it will give you a place to stand in addressing the questions.

> WHEN YOU TAKE YOURSELF OUT OF THE CENTER AND PUT GOD THERE, IT MAKES ALL THE DIFFERENCE WHAT KIND OF GOD YOU PUT THERE.

And that leads directly to the second discovery—the need to be absolutely honest with your questions. By now you can tell that I have placed several recurring themes into this book. The repetition is deliberate. Honesty is one theme. I have encountered people who thought their faith would be suspect unless they "put on a happy face" and pretended things were okay. But when some of those folks have been honest with me, they told me that this approach was never satisfactory. And a few of them confessed that glossing over their honesty only caused the doubt to fester underneath the surface.

I've come to view honesty as resembling the pain chart doctors and nurses use for hospital patients. Not long ago, I saw one on the wall of a patient's room. On one side was a smiley face with "no pain" written underneath it. At the other end was a contorted face with "the worst possible pain" underneath it. When nurses came in to check on the patient, they would ask how much pain she was in. Her choice determined the treatment. Likewise, in prayer, if we lose honesty with ourselves and our situation, we determine how much assistance we are willing to receive from the Great Physician. I've known people who refused to acknowledge their anger or frustration with intercessory prayer; consequently, I could never talk with them about it or counsel them to open themselves to God regarding it. Nothing good ever comes from such denial.

If you haven't read *A Grief Observed* by C. S. Lewis, I urge you to do so. When Lewis's beloved wife, Joy, died of cancer, he entered a deep depression. For a time he lost the sense of God's presence and questioned his faith in ways he had never done before. It was not a pretty picture, but it was real. Lewis spoke and wrote honestly about his feelings. He never completely understood why things had gone the way they had, but he did get back on his feet and regained spiritual stability in the face of his great loss. His book recounts that experience. Page after page resounds with honesty and, as a result, rings with truth.

What's interesting about honesty is that we always pray honestly on the front end of a situation. We tell God exactly what we want and how we feel. When we do not receive what we have asked for, we do not have to change the way we pray. We can continue to tell God exactly how we feel. God does not change. The same God who could receive our requests in the beginning can deal with our frustrations in the end. C. S. Lewis exemplifies this kind of praying. And as I have taken this lesson into the lives of many other people, I have found the same thing to be true.

This leads to my third discovery—the realization that the people of God over the ages have consistently practiced intercession. Intercessory prayer runs through every day of the Judeo-Christian tradition. The saints prayed for others, and they did so believing they were doing something that pleased God and had meaning. As with C. S. Lewis's experience, many of these men and women practiced intercessory prayer under discouraging circumstances. But the story of the church is one of unending intercession. When we pray for others, we step into a stream of prayer that has been flowing for at least four thousand years. There is value in keeping company with that cloud of witnesses.

Jesus is the ultimate example of intercessory prayer. He devoted his public ministry to praying for others. He prayed for all sorts of situations. He even prayed for others while hanging on the cross. But what really caught my attention was that when he ascended into heaven, he sat down at the right hand of God the Father to continue the priestly ministry of intercessory prayer (Heb. 7:25). At the same time, the Holy Spirit was sent to us, and the Spirit's ministry included interceding for us (Rom. 8:26-27). Consequently, when I pray for others, I not only follow in the steps of the saints, but also I practice a ministry that flows from the very heart of God.

This means that we find our best guidance and help from those who have prayed long and well for others. It is a mistake to draw conclusions about intercessory prayer from skeptics. We don't do that with any other aspect of life. We want to learn from the best examples, not the worst ones. Why should prayer be any different? We must enroll in the school of prayer that is taught by those who have devoted themselves to praying for others. When we do, we will receive wise counsel and practical advice. We can find some of these teachers in church history, and reading devotional classics plays a valuable role in our spiritual formation. Other teachers are still alive and writing well about intercessory prayer today. Some are people we can connect with for ongoing edification, and our choice of effective teachers does not have to be limited to a few "prayer celebrities" or perceived "prayer warriors." Paying attention to ordinary believers who live in a manner similar to the way we do often yields the greatest benefits.

A fourth discovery lies in learning to pray your heart's desire. A woman said to me in a prayer conference, "I don't always know what to pray for, and I don't want to pray for the wrong thing." I asked her, "Do you ever fail to know what you want when you pray for someone else?" She replied, "Oh, no. I always know what I'd like to see happen; I'm just not sure if what I want is what God wants." I responded, "Why don't you pray about the part you know and then leave the rest to God?" She concluded, "I never thought about that!"

I wanted her to think about that, and I want you to think about it too. I have stood by the bedsides of many people whose outcomes I did not know, but I did know what I desired for them. I've prayed for countless situations, having no idea how they would turn out, but I always had an idea of how I would like for them to turn out. So I pray my heart's desire. But I do so in a way that does not set the person I'm praying for up for despair if God doesn't answer exactly the way I'm praying. And I pray in a way that does not limit my ability to see God's hand at work. This is so important that I want to give you an actual example of such praying in relation to healing.

> Dear God, I come to you in this moment, praying for Tom. Our heart's desire is that he be healed from this cancer. We know there are many ways for him to be healed, and we do not want to exclude any of those ways, including the healing that sometimes comes in death. What we want you to know, above everything else, is that we know you are a God who heals, and we trust you to heal Tom in the way that is in accordance with your will. As you do this, we pray that you will come near to Tom and minister grace to him. And what we ask for him, we ask for ourselves as well. In the name of Jesus. Amen.

This prayer keeps the focus on God, but it does so in the context of faith and in the realm of trust. We have not limited God or set Tom up to believe that God only has one way to heal him. But we have prayed our heart's desire. We have not held back in telling God precisely what we would like to see happen. Nevertheless, we are praying in a way that does not make us the definers of Tom's disease or God's grace. God is sovereign, and Tom is in God's care. It's okay.

I believe God delights in this kind of praying. Most of all, we allow God to be in control—which the Almighty really is, whether or not we pray like it. But we also pray in a way that does not require us to know God's specific will in advance. We can pray now. We can pray our heart's desire without hesitation or fear. Out of this kind of praying comes a marvelous discovery: our hearts become one with God's heart, because we both want the best for Tom. We are not praying in a way that hopes to find God's needle in the haystack, but rather in a way that affirms, "Thy kingdom come. Thy will be done in earth as it is in heaven." That is a very good way to pray.

Such intercession puts prayer in the right arrangement. Our part is to pray; God's part is to weave everything into the tapestry of the divine will. Yes, we're back to mystery, and this kind of praying does not leave us without some questions or struggles. But it is the kind of praying that enables us to know we have prayed aright. We have prayed, believing that God works for good, and that somehow those for whom we pray will be cared for by God's love. We may not see that happen here on earth, but we have not limited our understanding of answers to this world. As Philip Yancey puts it, we are those who have believed the "rumors of another world," so we pray in relation to both worlds and leave it to God to act in either one.

> OUR PART IS TO PRAY; GOD'S PART IS TO WEAVE EVERYTHING INTO THE TAPESTRY OF THE DIVINE WILL.

This kind of praying also helps us determine how long to pray about a particular matter. I'm convinced there are situations we will pray about all our lives, but not every intercession has to last for years or even be expressed every single day. When we have spoken to God about the person or matter, it is enough. We can rest in that knowledge. We can leave it with God. This does not mean we will not honor the promptings of the Spirit to pray again about some people or things, but it does mean we will not be driven to keep on praying by a deceiving fear that says, "You must pray more . . . and more . . . and more; otherwise, God will not answer."

What makes prayer authentic is not how many times you say the prayer but rather that you see that part of life in relation to God. Of course, you will pray repeatedly about some things. But for other situations, it will be sufficient to pray once and move on. I often tell people to use the "broken-record syndrome" as a guide. When you find yourself merely repeating words you've used before—when you find yourself unable to add anything new to the prayer—then trust that you have told God everything you need to say for the time being. Don't become a broken record. Your heart will almost always let you know the difference.

A fifth discovery comes in what we might call the management of prayer. The mystery and magnitude of prayer can overwhelm us if we are not careful. I have noticed that prayer teachers find a way to organize their prayers. For example, John Wesley divided his intercessions over a seven-day cycle. Each day had a particular focus, both with respect to subjects for which to pray and to the cultivation of one particular virtue in life. When you look at his prayer cycle, it would be possible to believe that each theme and each life quality could (or should) be prayed for each day. But as others before and since have known, Wesley realized that to stack everything up into one day, and to do that every day, would be to weaken prayer rather than to strengthen it. So, he established a prayer pattern that enabled him to pray about many things over a reasonable period of time. I think he was able to do this because he realized that he was a creature of time, but God is not. To pray genuinely one day a week about certain matters is okay. God receives it as true prayer, and we practice it with a pace of grace that makes our praying more meaningful.

For years, my personal pattern has been to use a weekly cycle with people and topics recurring once a week. In addition, I pray for certain people and ministries one day a month, usually simply calling their names and recalling their influence in my life. Finally, I keep a monthly prayer list to which I add circumstances that arise during that month. I usually carry over to the next month only a few items that still seem to need continuing intercession. Once in a while, I will turn to other prayer cycles and include them in my intercession. For example, as I write this, I am using a prayer guide to pray for military personnel. In times past, I have used other guides to prayer from Protestant, Roman Catholic, and Orthodox traditions. I do this as a way of ensuring that I am praying with the whole church, not just my preferred part of it.

Weaving its way throughout my intercession is my growing comfort in praying the scriptures back to God. The Bible is full of intercessory prayers. As I become familiar with them, I find that some of them fit the situations of people for whom I want to pray. It is natural to use those prayers as I lift up the needs of others. In this way, the Bible becomes a prayer book. When we use scripture in this way, we move into, through, and out of God's Word in a different but meaningful fashion. Sometimes I find that praying the Word gives me a perspective on my intercession that I would not have if I had limited my praying to my own words.

All such matters fall into the larger category of prayer management for me. I came to the point where this was absolutely necessary. Every morning I was trying to read the Bible devotionally, to read other devotional works, and still pray for my complete prayer list. It simply was not working. And when I realized it, it was as if the saints of the ages smiled and said to one another, "He's finally getting it!" I want you to "get it" too.

Most of all, I want you to develop a heart for intercessory prayer. I believe it is an expression of God's heart for the world. I also believe that intercessory prayer is the best way to rise above self-centeredness. Years ago, Dr. Tom Carruth told me that Frank Laubach, the famous missionary and father of the modern literacy movement, began each day praying, "God, what are you doing in the world today that I can help you with?" It was Laubach's way of connecting to that larger will and work and being an instrument in the hands of God. Similarly, E. Stanley Jones called his morning devotions "going to the listening post." He went there to receive his marching orders for the day. Thomas Merton taught that intercessory prayer was the igniting element for a social consciousness. And Evelyn Underhill revealed how intercession was at the heart of mysticism, which far from being a detached self was, in fact, a consecrated self.

Intercessory prayer may be the most difficult part of prayer to understand, but it is not the most difficult to practice. Just pray for others. Tell God what your heart tells you to say about them. I believe that if you are a devoted disciple of Jesus, the Holy Spirit will dispose your heart to pray for others in a way that glorifies God, honors your own sense of honesty, and makes a difference. Here's a suggestion: use the time you might normally spend trying to figure out intercessory prayer to pray for others. The indwelling Christ will honor your commitment, for his presence is an interceding presence. As you pray for others, God will move you away from self-centeredness. The ascended Christ will nudge you to do what he does for others—pray for them. And before long, you will discover that intercession is not only a form of prayer but a way of life.

The same God who inspires us to pray for others will also move us to act on their behalf. And then we will have discovered what praying for others is all about.

CHAPTER 8
PRAYING FOR YOURSELF

Prayer is not only the "lifting up of the mind and heart to God," but it is also the response to God within us, the discovery of God within us; it leads ultimately to the discovery and fulfillment of our own true being in God.

—THOMAS MERTON

Beth spoke out in a workshop: "I need to know how to pray about me." She remarked that she was weary of praying "give me, get me" prayers. She sensed there must be more to prayer than that, but she was not sure what. Her comments reminded me of the comic strip *Pogo*, whose main character spoke these words, "We have met the enemy . . . and he is us!" That exclamation can apply to prayer. We feel as though we're talking in the dark when we pray for ourselves as much as we do when we approach prayer in relation to the other issues we've examined.

We know it's okay to pray for ourselves. Jesus told us to ask, seek, and knock (Matt. 7:7). The Bible is full of stories in which people prayed for themselves. The Psalms are particularly full of prayers lifted up by men and women who were quite specific in naming things they wanted for themselves. Whatever else we may say about it, praying for ourselves is a legitimate type of prayer. So why the darkness?

I think it has to do with a fundamental misunderstanding of the self. We feel strange praying for ourselves, because we have a secular, rather than a biblical, notion of the self. The secular notion tells me I am an independent, individual self that is supposed to be affirmed and actualized. In other words, we are egocentric. We focus on ourselves and become set on having things our way. We want what we want when we want it. But we were not made to think or live that way. That's why Beth felt that "give me, get me" prayers are inadequate. That's why we sense that there must be something more. The Bible clearly says there is. Instead of the psychologized understanding that I am a self, the Bible teaches that I am a person. And there is a profound difference in how we pray, depending on whether we view our lives as selves or as persons. To be a person is to be like God, who is a Person. And this likeness to God (*imago dei*) is the starting point for praying for ourselves.

Fundamentally, *imago dei* means that I am a being in relation to others. That's the line of demarcation between viewing my life as a self or as a person. As a self, it is possible to understand life in isolation. But when I realize that I am a person, I understand that I am always in community. I think that's the reason the Lord's Prayer begins with the word *Our*. We cannot pray as independent, isolated, self-actualizing individuals. We are persons in relation to other persons. Primarily we are persons related to God. Then we are persons related to one another. Therefore, I will pray for myself with the spirit that says, "God, I ask only those things for myself that will glorify you and make me a fuller and finer member of the human family."

When I was twelve or thirteen, my dad gave me a little book by Edgar A. Guest titled *You Can't Live Your Own Life.* When he gave it to me, he told me it was one of his favorite books, and he had tried to pattern his life after it. You can guess the book's basic message from the title. Guest, a well-known newspaper reporter, had interviewed people from all walks of life for a long time. He discovered that the happiest, best, and most contributive people were those who knew they could not live selfishly. It was a journalist's way of trying to tell the world what the Bible has been saying all along.

Following closely on the heels of this misunderstanding of self is the problem related to our understanding of God. I will hesitate to pray for myself if I view God as either unwilling or unable to hear and respond. I will especially hesitate to pray for myself if I think that my request may somehow upset God. I will play it safe. That's why the Lord's Prayer has the word *Father* as its second word. The One to whom we pray is the one who made us, loves us, and wants to do more for us than we can ask or imagine. Jesus dealt with this idea when he reminded us that human parents would never give their children a snake instead of a fish or a scorpion instead of an egg (Luke 11:11-12). Neither will God fail to give good things to those who ask.

Praying for myself in relation to "Father" also means I am confessing that my viewpoint is not the only way of looking at things. God may hear my prayer and deal with it in a way I never could have imagined. I learned this lesson from my dad as well. I was going through an "I want to be an airplane pilot" phase. In a catalog I had seen a toy that looked like a cockpit dashboard. It had all the dials, throttles, and steering wheel of a real plane. I hinted more than once that I would really like to have that toy.

Not long afterward, I went with my mom to visit my grandmother. We were gone for about a week. When we returned home, Dad was there to meet us. He asked me to close my eyes and led me through the house into the backyard. When I opened my eyes, I saw a complete wooden airplane (child-sized) sitting there. While I had been away, Dad had gone to the lumberyard, purchased wood, and built me a working airplane that had a steering stick and pedals that made the ailerons on the wings and tail move back and forth. I never thought about the toy I'd seen in the catalog again, but I spent hundreds of hours flying my "new and improved" airplane. My dad had done better than I ever could have imagined. When I pray to "Father," I am praying to the One who knows best.

> To say that God is "in heaven" does not mean God is distant or aloof.

I'm also glad to know that my Father is "in heaven." When I pray for myself, I pray against the backdrop of the eternal and the unchanging. Nothing I see on earth matches that. I want to pray in relation to those things which are utterly secure and dependable. To say that God is "in heaven" does not mean God is distant or aloof. Rather, it was Jesus' way of teaching us that God is dependable, and that answers to our prayers come from that dimension of life where change and corruption do not reign. When we pray for ourselves, we can say, "God, please answer my prayer in a way that further aligns me with the eternal realities to which you want my life to conform." And that's why we go on to say, "Thy kingdom come. Thy will be done in earth, as it is in heaven." I've come to believe that "Thy will be done" is the most important phrase in the Lord's Prayer. It is the defining element. Rather than being egocentric selves, we are persons abandoned to God—people who want God's will to be done, not their own. We pray for ourselves as consecrated and yielded selves. That's what it means to hallow God's name and to desire God's will to be done on earth as it is in heaven.

These opening words and phrases of the Lord's Prayer provide the perspective out of which we pray for ourselves. They set the boundaries that enable us to then move into making specific requests for ourselves. You have probably noticed that the rest of the Lord's Prayer contains "us" phrases. It is not an intercessory prayer; it is a prayer we pray for ourselves, but the "us" phrases are correct and safe only when preceded by the view of God and ourselves that the first section of the prayer provides. When they are firmly planted in our hearts, we can pray for ourselves with the confidence that we are praying in keeping with the Lord's Prayer.

We can say to God, "Give us." We are no longer self-centered selves making this request but persons intent on glorifying God and enriching the human family.

Jesus tells us that what we need is "daily bread." This phrase contains several important ideas. First, the bread is for this day. When the Israelites wandered in the wilderness, God fed them with manna in daily installments, except on the sixth day. The people were instructed to gather only enough manna for the day. Stockpiling or hoarding was forbidden. Similarly, when we pray for ourselves, we pray for our lives as they are here and now. We do not try to pray as a way to reverse the past or presume the future. We pray in a way that honors the present moment, believing that God will link the days of our lives into a larger chain that will span our time here on earth.

Moreover, the bread we pray for is fresh. Archaeologists unearthed a grocery list that contained the same Greek phrase we translate "daily bread." It was probably written by a wife or mother to a spouse or child, telling the person going to the store to be sure to get the bread that had been baked fresh that day, not day-old bread. When we apply that concept to prayer, it means that God's best food for our souls is "fresh food," not gifts we have allowed to grow stale. Memories are good to cherish, but they cannot feed us today. When we pray for daily bread, we ask God to give us a fresh taste of divine provision.

We pray for the bread we need, not necessarily all the bread we want. That is, we pray as stewards, not consumers. When we say, "Give us," we are not asking for everything. We ask God to provide what we need for the life we are called to live. As I've studied the prayer lives of the saints, I've discovered that while they prayed general prayers, they also grew in the sense that God had given them particular things to pray for. They had a kind of divine prayer list; they had been given some specific prayer assignments. They did much of their praying in relation to that more particular and focused sense—the bread they needed, the bread God wanted them to have.

I'm sure you've experienced this. It is one thing to pray for God's blessing on missionaries. It's another matter to pray for a particular missionary, and even more meaningful to pray for a missionary who is a close friend or relative. For years, I have encouraged people to pray their lives—to pray about the things that touch them most deeply. If we have the kind of heart I've described previously, we do not need to worry about becoming selfish in our praying. God will put the parts of the world into our hearts that need to be there. But at the same time, we will discover the joy in praying for ourselves those things that are most personal and meaningful to us.

We also pray, "Forgive us." Our generation does not use words like *sin* and *guilt* to describe our dilemmas. But whatever we call them, we spend billions of dollars each year on medication and counseling to help us get over our problems. Many of the addictive behaviors that plague people mask a deeper sense of emptiness and estrangement. No matter what we may name our demons, we are a people who need to be forgiven.

This is where great good news comes pouring into our lives as we pray for ourselves. God waits to forgive us! All we have to do is ask! It's not waving a magic wand, and not everything we ask to be forgiven of is taken care of instantly. In fact, God may respond to our prayers for forgiveness by asking us to exert all the effort we can and get whatever help we need. But we are invited in the Lord's Prayer to pray for ourselves in relation to forgiveness.

GOD WILL PUT THE PARTS OF THE WORLD INTO OUR HEARTS THAT NEED TO BE THERE.

Notice the interesting twist, "Forgive us our trespasses *as we forgive those who trespass against us.*" The little adverb *as* is interesting and sheds light on how we pray for forgiveness. For one thing, it means that our ability to accept God's forgiveness is related to our willingness to forgive others. I've noticed that those who hold grudges tend to be difficult people with crusty dispositions. Such a countenance is harder for God to break through to give forgiveness. If we replace *as* with *like*, the prayer may mean that we will receive God's forgiveness to the extent and manner in which we are willing to forgive others. Finally, *as* may indicate a conjoining of the divine and the human so that the life of extending and receiving forgiveness is a whole, not two separate parts. In whatever ways these meanings come to us, the good news is that we do not have to live with the weight of the past crashing down upon us. We can be set free. It's always appropriate to pray for forgiveness.

And then Jesus teaches us to say, "Lead us not into temptation." For most of us, that's the most confusing part of the prayer. The idea of God *leading* anyone into temptation strikes us as contrary to everything we know about "Father" or the way God works (James 1:13). We're on target to doubt the phrase as it is written, but that's precisely the problem—it is written in a language we no longer speak. When people in seventeenth-century England prayed "not into," they meant "away from." When you make that substitution, the prayer becomes clear and important, for it invites us to say, "lead us *away from* temptation." I don't know about you, but I think that's a great request to make for yourself.

I'm old enough to have had friends who went astray; a few did so in dramatic ways, bringing suffering and shame on those around them. But all of them had a "first day" of temptation—a moment when the temptation resembled a flicker more than a fire, or a pesky fly more than a savage beast. Every temptation can be dealt with when it is like that. But when the temptation is not resisted, it grows. Jesus is saying, "Pray for yourself, that you will notice the earliest stirring of temptation—the weakest flame—and ask God to lead you away from it."

One of my favorite prayer requests is Psalm 139:23-24: "Search me, O God, and know my heart; test me and know my thoughts. See if there is any wicked way in me, and lead me in the way everlasting." David prayed this prayer out of the sad experience of having yielded to temptation in a tragic way. So he set God as a guard to the doorway of his heart, asking God to perpetually search, test, and know his heart. We would all do well to post that kind of sentry over our lives.

But there's more. Thanks to a professor friend, I learned that the word *wicked* can also mean "hurtful." When I discovered that definition, it put David's prayer in an entirely new light. Previously when I had prayed this prayer, I contented myself with the knowledge that I passed the "wicked test" most days. But when I substituted the word *hurtful*, things were different. When I prayed, "See if there is any hurtful way in me," the Holy Spirit responded, "Steve, I'm glad you asked. We need to talk." And the Spirit brought to my remembrance some word or deed that caused someone else pain. You see, I have to pray about myself in relation to things like that. I am not free to ignore the smallest temptations or the lightest afflictions I cause others. Whenever I act in a way that hurts God, myself, or others, I must pray about that.

But I do not always do this in time. Sometimes I have already fallen into the pit before I muster the willingness to call for help. That's where the phrase "deliver us" comes into play. I can be led away from temptation before I have yielded to it, but when I pray for deliverance, my feet are already in the fire. I am already in the hole before I decide to get out of it. If "deliver us from evil" were not in the prayer, I would have to put it there, because at times I do not heed God's warnings, and all I can do is cry out for is God's rescue.

As the early church moved beyond Jerusalem into the rest of the world, devoted disciples sinned, and the rest of the

Christian community had to deal with the resulting devastation. Paul captured the spirit of the Lord's Prayer when he wrote these words to the Galatians: "My friends, if anyone is detected in a transgression, you who have received the Spirit should restore such a one in a spirit of gentleness" (6:1). The word translated "restore" is a Greek term used to describe the process of setting a broken bone. Even in our brokenness there is hope. God supplies grace to "deliver us" and often prescribes for that grace to flow to us through the loving acts of fellow believers.

> GOD SUPPLIES GRACE TO "DELIVER US" AND OFTEN PRESCRIBES FOR THAT GRACE TO FLOW TO US THROUGH THE LOVING ACTS OF FELLOW BELIEVERS.

If you talk with a doctor, you'll discover that when a bone heals at the breaking point, it becomes stronger than it was before the break happened. The same holds true with God's rescue from evil. We will become stronger at our breaking point, because we know we were once broken right there, and because we have experienced the restoration God can provide.

Part of the reason prayer seems like talking in the dark is because we have dwelled so long in the darkness that we forget what it was to live in the light. I saw this in a man named Charles, to whom some of us had been ministering on the streets of Lexington, Kentucky. One night he didn't show up at the place we'd agreed to meet. I walked around the corner and found him dead drunk in a bar booth—so drunk that when he saw me and stood up, he flung his beer all over me. Greatly embarrassed, he nearly ran outside as I followed him. "Leave me alone!" he exclaimed. "I am going to hell, and there is nothing you or anyone else can do about it. You don't really know me. I deserve to go there." That night he was talking from a darkness deeper than I had ever seen in another person. Nothing I said made any difference; after a few minutes he waved his hand in a "get out of here" gesture and went back inside the bar. My last words to him before he disappeared were, "I am going to keep praying for you." And I have—a thousand times.

It does not have to be that way for you. You can pray for yourself, "deliver me." *Despair* is not the final word in the Christian's vocabulary; *hope* is. This prayer is offered to us precisely when we are in the evil—when it has its grip on us—when nothing we have done is enough. God is still there. I have no idea if you need that kind of prayer for yourself, but I had to include it in this book, because Jesus put it in the Lord's Prayer. If you need to pray "deliver me," do so right now. Nothing can separate you from the love of God in Christ Jesus. Stop and read the eighth chapter of Romans. You will see that there is no act or attitude, no matter how evil, from which God is not willing to deliver you. You can pray for God to deliver you, and you can ask the Christian community to join you in praying.

Beth was right, wasn't she? We can pray a lot more for ourselves than "give me, get me" prayers. God opens the way for a vast array of personal prayers—prayers that will make all the difference in our lives, which of course will make a difference in others' lives as well. Is it any wonder that the Lord's Prayer ends as it began—with God back in the center of the picture:

"for thine is the kingdom, and the power, and the glory, for ever"? There's no better way to pray for yourself than to end up in the arms of God. It's the place where everything ends with a hearty "Amen!"

EPILOGUE

If you gain, you gain all. If you lose, you lose nothing.
Wager then, without hesitation, that [God] exists.

—BLAISE PASCAL

Sound travels in darkness as well as light. You can talk in the dark. You can pray in the dark too—the darkness of uncertainty, confusion, and failure. You can pray when life doesn't make sense. That's the golden thread I've tried to weave through every page of this book. I told you at the start that I had only one goal: to deal as honestly with prayer as I could and yet leave you, at the end, still wanting to pray. I hope and pray I have done that.

When people asked me what I was writing about and I gave them the title, I went on to say, "It's my Philip Yancey book." If you have read any of Yancey's writing, you know what I mean. He has a God-given ability to shoot straight on almost any issue, but he does so in such a manner that your faith is strengthened in the process. That has been my aim every time I wrote a paragraph: to communicate honesty and to instill hope. I also think of this as my Philip Yancey book because he frequently refers to faith as "The Wager."[1] It really is. And I believe that phrase accurately paraphrases the Bible's definition of faith in Hebrews 11:1: "Now faith is the assurance of things hoped for, the conviction of things not seen."

For me, that's also a perfect definition of prayer: assurance of things hoped for, conviction of things not seen. Prayer is faith talking—sometimes talking in the dark, when all you can do is hope for things not seen. Prayer puts words to the great wager. So what keeps prayer from being a spiritual crapshoot? Just one factor: you're talking in the dark to God. Put God into any equation, situation, idea, or question, and the whole thing changes. Perhaps that is why someone long ago coined the phrase "Prayer changes things"—because that person knew that God changes things, and prayer is conversation with God.

But some people who read this book will reach this page and say, "Not true. Prayer didn't change anything for me." I must take seriously your response and treat it tenderly, for if you feel that way, you do so out of some kind of deep pain. We don't agonize over bruises but over lost limbs.

If you have read to this point and still are moved to say, "Prayer didn't change anything for me," at least I hope you know I have not tried to avoid you or your exclamation. I have not tried to exclude you and your experience from this book. And my response is that while prayer may not have changed your circumstances, it changed one thing: it put those circumstances in a different context. By that, I mean,your circumstances (and mine) do not have the last word. If we cling tenaciously to the revelation of scripture, we hold on to the fact that God has the last word. It's one reason why there must be a new heaven and a new earth. The ones we have now are not adequate to explain or contain everything.

All I can really ask you to do, and all I can do, is to keep praying when life doesn't make sense—to keep praying in the face of insufficient evidence that prayer "works." I appeal to you to base your beliefs about prayer on revelation, not speculation; on the long haul, not the short run; on heaven and earth combined, not earth alone. If you continue to talk in the dark and pray when life doesn't make sense, you will be no farther behind in the life of prayer than the greatest saint. Those women and men who prayed before us left footprints that go through the deepest valleys as well as the mountaintops.

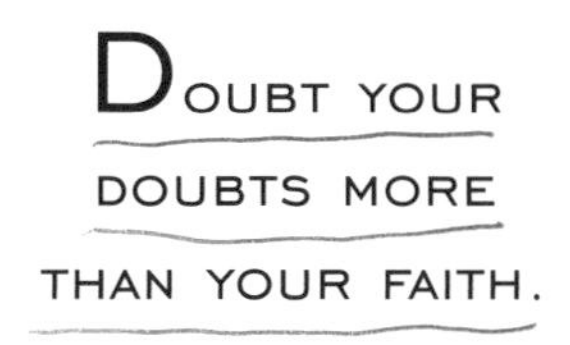

As I bring this book to a close, I'm going to ask you to do something strange: *doubt your doubts more than your faith.* Isn't it interesting how we normally doubt our faith? Why don't we doubt our doubts? Why do we gravitate toward tearing down our picture of God and replacing it with a picture of ourselves? I have come to think that this is the supreme temptation, and if the evil one can succeed here, the ripple effect will occur in almost every other area of our lives. So I'm asking you to doubt your doubts and hold on to your faith. Cling to revelation. And if you are like me, that will mean reading the Story (scripture) over and over again—and continuing to read it when life doesn't make sense. To borrow Garrison Keillor's question and apply it to the Message, "If this is not true, what else might not be true?"

But if it is true, then whether or not life makes sense, we have hope. People who pray "nevertheless" are explorers more than philosophers. They keep going, even against the odds. At the same time, explorers are not Pollyanna people who construct their own la-la land and live there. Explorers know more about life than ivory-tower folks ever will. Give me a person off the road rather than a book off the shelf every time. The same holds true for prayer. Give me great souls who have been knocked off their feet by life rather than detached sages who merely speculate about life. Give me a saint who tells me how difficult it is to keep praying rather than a Christian celebrity who tells me prayer is easy and gets results. I'm asking you to believe things that are hard to believe, but if you stop believing, what else might not be true?

In doing the research for this book, I became fascinated with a kind of prayer that has virtually disappeared. The Bible calls it lament. It is prayer that occurs precisely when life doesn't make sense. Lament takes place in the middle of loss—when we realize that situations will not return to what they once were. There's a whole book of Lamentations in the Bible, but once you've seen the concept, you will find that kind of praying in other places as well. Lament is the kind of praying that comes through tears. It is praying when all you can do is weep. We need to recover the lost language of lament. For some of us, it may become a primary prayer language. It is a language spoken in the dark. It is "nevertheless" praying.

Every time we pray, we declare that there is more to life than we know or can figure out. We affirm that God and God's ways are more real than the things we can verify by our senses. Rather than giving up and deciding to live in the "real world," those who pray are convinced that prayer is the language of the Real World. Time-bound people will never understand us, and they will continue to call us naive. But we can take that criticism; it surely isn't the worst thing life can throw at us.

Prayer demonstrates our conviction that God exists, God matters, God cares, and God has the final word over every individual life and over life itself. Life ends with death on Friday; prayer carries us to resurrection on Sunday. Notice that I wrote "carries us," for there are times when we cannot make it to resurrection unless we are taken there. Prayer is precisely for the times when we can only hope for things we do not see.

The world will say God is silent, but we have a book full of God's words. The world will say God is not fair, but we have never believed that fairness is the definition of life. The world will say that God is hidden, but we believe we have seen God in the face of Jesus Christ. Our convictions do not answer all the questions, nor do they eliminate all the mystery. But when compared to a view of life that makes us bitter, not better, we are willing to take the risk. We are willing to make the great wager.

In the final analysis, we *choose* to pray. We talk in the dark because we believe there is Someone to talk to—and to hear from. And according to this line of thinking, talking beats not talking every time. Faith beats cynicism. Hope is better than despair. Even when things don't make sense or turn out okay, we believe it is still better to pray than not to pray. We believe this because we have abandoned the belief that everything has to be worked out and made right in this world. There's not enough time for that to happen, so God has also made eternity for us to live in. Prayer keeps us facing into and moving toward eternity.

Revelation is not my favorite book of the Bible, and in my opinion some of the worst theology created has been based on it. I do not use Revelation to predict the future or interpret every event. But I do believe Revelation is part of God's Word, and I have discovered that this book can enable us to pray well—to keep talking in the dark. It provides the perspective that God, and nothing else, will have the last word about everything—including everything we call bad, wrong, or unfair. God will speak the final word over it all, and that word will sound something like this:

> Then the angel showed me the river of the water of life, bright as crystal, flowing from the throne of God and of the Lamb. . . . Nothing accursed will be found there. . . . And there will be no more night; they need no light of lamp or sun, for the Lord God will be their light. . . .
>
> And [the angel] said to me, "These words are trustworthy and true." (Revelation 22:1, 3, 5, 6)

And so we keep talking in the dark. Sound travels both in darkness and in light.

QUESTIONS

FOR REFLECTION AND DISCUSSION

PRELUDE TO PART ONE

Write a prayer about anything currently affecting your life. Make it at least one page so it includes some detail. Read back over your prayer and reflect on these questions:

- What picture of God comes through?
- What picture of yourself is evident in this prayer?
- How does the church show up in this prayer?
- What are the main emotions in the prayer?

CHAPTER 1: The God Problem Let God be God

1. Which of the God problems mentioned in this chapter most concerns you?

2. What picture of God does this chapter paint for you?

3. The author says that in order to continue to pray, we must learn to live with mystery. Where does mystery fit into your prayer life? God's Ways are higher than our ways. Trust

4. When have you chosen to pray in the midst of your questions? Randy's death.

5. When have you had an experience of total honesty in prayer such as Mary had in this chapter? Describe.
6. What insights on "doubting Thomas" have you received from this chapter?

Chapter 2: The Human Problem

1. Where have you seen examples of "magical" beliefs about prayer?
2. When have you exchanged the question "how me?" for "why me?" What difference did it make in your perspective?
3. How have you experienced the difference between artificial and authentic prayer?
4. In what ways have you or others you know experienced "joy in perspective"?

Chapter 3: The Church Problem

1. What is your experience of prayer meetings in church?
2. In what ways does your church undersell or oversell prayer?
3. How does a "talking" image of prayer (versus "breathing") help you?
4. What images arise when you think of the church as a house of prayer? How might your church create a more prayerful atmosphere?

CHAPTER 4: Nevertheless

1. What does "nevertheless" prayer add to your prayer life? How does it keep you talking in the dark?

2. How does Jesus' "nevertheless" prayer in the garden of Gethsemane relate to your prayer life?

3. How does a theology of heaven put your prayers into a different context?

4. How have you experienced God's companionship in "the valley of the shadow of death" (Ps. 23:4, KJV)?

5. What scripture or hymn most encourages you to stay the course in prayer?

CHAPTER 5: Praying When You're Dry

1. When have you experienced deep spiritual dryness, like that of Charles (pp. 65–67)? To whom did you talk about the experience?

2. How has spiritual dryness affected your prayer life? Did you keep praying through dry times?

3. Where is your prayer life on the spectrum of honesty in prayer?

4. What insights do you draw from Asaph's story?

5. How do you identify with the causes of spiritual dryness mentioned on pages 69 and 74–75?

CHAPTER 6: Praying When Life Suddenly Changes

1. When have you had to pray after being blindsided by life?
2. How do you respond to the idea that sometimes prayer is not a way "out" but rather a way "through"?
3. How are you digging deep "grace wells" to draw from when life suddenly changes?
4. Who have you known that showed remarkable grace in the face of crisis? What did you learn from that person?

CHAPTER 7: Praying for Others

1. How do you handle the unknown in your praying?
2. How is intercession affected when we put God, not ourselves, at the center?
3. What might it mean for you to pray honestly—from start to finish?
4. How might you "pray your heart's desire" in relation to your life right now?
5. How have you avoided becoming overwhelmed in your prayers of intercession?

CHAPTER 8: Praying for Yourself

1. How has your prayer moved from self-centeredness without taking yourself out of the picture?
2. What insights emerge when you replace *self* with *person*?

3. What have you learned about using the Lord's Prayer as a guide to prayer, not just as a prayer to pray?

Epilogue

1. How will reading this book change your prayer life?
2. How is it possible for you to doubt your doubts more than your faith?
3. What is your experience with the prayer of lament?

NOTES

PROLOGUE

Epigraph. Frederick Buechner, *Beyond Words: Daily Readings in the ABC's of Faith* (San Francisco: HarperSanFrancisco, 2004), 267.

PART ONE: Foundations

Epigraph. David L. McKenna, *Journey Through a Bypass: The Story of an Open Heart* (Indianapolis: Light & Life Communications, 1998), 53.

CHAPTER 1: The God Problem

Epigraph. Emilie Griffin, *Clinging: The Experience of Prayer* (San Francisco: Harper & Row, 1984), 9.

1. Joseph M. Scriven, "What a Friend We Have in Jesus," *The United Methodist Hymnal* (Nashville: United Methodist Publishing House, 1989), no. 526.

2. Maxie Dunnam, *Unless We Pray* (Nashville: Upper Room Books, 1998), vi.

CHAPTER 2: The Human Problem

Epigraph. Marie T. Freeman, quoted in *A Woman's Treasury of Faith* (Grand Rapids, MI: Family Christian Press, 2004), 14.

CHAPTER 3: The Church Problem

Epigraph. Jonathan L. Graf and Lani C. Hinkle, eds., *My*

House Shall Be a House of Prayer (Colorado Springs: NavPress Publishing Group, 2001), 4.

CHAPTER 4: Nevertheless!
Epigraph. Sophie Scholl, quoted in Johann Christoph Arnold, *Cries from the Heart: Stories of Struggle and Hope* (Maryknoll, NY: Orbis Books, 2004).

1. Maltbie D. Babcock, "This Is My Father's World," *The United Methodist Hymnal*, no. 144.

PART TWO: Expressions
Epigraph. O. Hallesby, *Prayer* (London: Inter-Varsity Fellowship, 1962), 38.

CHAPTER 5: Praying When You're Dry
Epigraph. Corrie ten Boom, quoted in *A Woman's Treasury of Faith*, 15.

CHAPTER 6: Praying When Life Suddenly Changes
Epigraph. Original quotation from Julian of Norwich, *Showings*, trans. Edmund Colledge and James Walsh, Classics of Western Spirituality Series (New York: Paulist Press, 1978), 315. Updated language found in *A Woman's Treasury of Hope* (Grand Rapids, MI: Family Christian Press, 2004), 56.

CHAPTER 7: Praying for Others
Epigraph. Oswald Chambers, *My Utmost for His Highest* (Uhrichsville, OH: Barbour, n.d.), 90.

CHAPTER 8: Praying for Yourself
Epigraph. Thomas Merton, *A Call to Contemplation*, in

Christine M. Bochen, *Thomas Merton: Essential Writings* (Maryknoll, NY: Orbis Books, 2000), 82.

EPILOGUE

Epigraph. Blaise Pascal, *Pensées*, Section III, 233. Available at www.ccel.org.

1. Philip Yancey, *Disappointment with God* (Grand Rapids, MI: Zondervan, 1988), 308–10.

SUGGESTED READING

I recommend the following books as follow-up reading on prayer. Some titles are no longer in print, but the Internet contains ample means to find and purchase older materials.

Bloesch, Donald G. *The Struggle of Prayer*. Colorado Springs: Helmers & Howard Publishers, 1988.

Bloom, Anthony. *Beginning to Pray*. Farmington Hills, MI: Thomson Gale, 1986.

Bonhoeffer, Dietrich. *The Cost of Discipleship*. New York: Simon & Schuster, 1995.

Brother Lawrence. *The Practice of the Presence of God*. Peabody, MA: Hendrickson Publishers, 2004.

Card, Michael. *A Sacred Sorrow: Reaching Out to God in the Lost Language of Lament*. Colorado Springs: NavPress Publishing Group, 2005.

Chambers, Oswald. *If You Will Ask*. Fort Washington, PA: Christian Literature Crusade, 1985.

Douglas, Deborah Smith. *The Praying Life: Seeking God in All Things*. Harrisburg, PA: Morehouse Publishing, 2003.

Dunnam, Maxie. *The Workbook of Living Prayer*. Nashville: Upper Room Books, 1994.

Fosdick, Harry Emerson. *The Meaning of Prayer*. Whitefish, MT: Kessinger Publishing, 2005.

Foster, Richard J. *Prayer*. New York: HarperCollins Publishers, 2007.

Frost, Rob. *When I Can't Pray*. Eastbourne, Great Britain: Kingsway Publications, 2001.

Green, Thomas. *Drinking from a Dry Well: A Sequel to When the Well Runs Dry*. Notre Dame, IN: Ave Maria Press, 1991.

Griffin, Emilie. *Doors into Prayer: An Invitation*. Orleans, MA: Paraclete Press, 2005.

Hubbard, David Allan. *The Problem with Prayer Is . . .* Wheaton, IL: Tyndale House, 1972.

Jones, E. Stanley. *How to Pray*. Nashville: Abingdon Press, 1975.

Leech, Kenneth. *True Prayer: An Invitation to Christian Spirituality*. Harrisburg, PA: Morehouse Publishing, 1995.

LeFevre, Perry D. *Understandings of Prayer*. Louisville, KY: Westminster John Knox Press, 1981.

Lewis, C. S. *A Grief Observed*. San Francisco: Harper-SanFrancisco, 1994.

———. *Letters to Malcom: Chiefly on Prayer*. San Diego: Harcourt Trade Publishers, 2002.

Lockyer, Herbert. *All the Prayers of the Bible*. Grand Rapids, MI: Zondervan, 1990.

Merton, Thomas. *Contemplative Prayer*. Garden City, NY: Image Books, 1971.

Muto, Susan A., and Adrian van Kaam. *Practicing the Prayer of Presence*. Totowa, NJ: Resurrection Press, 1993.

Nouwen, Henri J. M. *The Only Necessary Thing: Living a Prayerful Life.* New York: Crossroad Publishing, 1999.

O'Connor, Elizabeth. *Cry Pain, Cry Hope: Thresholds to Purpose and Creativity.* Waco, TX: Word Books, 1987.

Steere, Douglas V. *Dimensions of Prayer.* Nashville: Upper Room Books, 2002.

Underhill, Evelyn. *Life as Prayer and Other Writings of Evelyn Underhill.* Edited by Lucy Menzies. Harrisburg, PA: Morehouse Publishing, 1991.

Wallis, Paul. *Rough Ways in Prayer: How Can I Pray When I Feel Spiritually Dead?* Nashville: Abingdon Press, 1995.

Yancey, Philip. *Disappointment with God: Three Questions No One Asks Aloud.* Grand Rapids, MI: Zondervan, 2006.

———. *Reaching for the Invisible God: What Can We Expect to Find?* Grand Rapids, MI: Zondervan, 2002.

PRAYER MINISTRY RESOURCES

The resources in this section can help you develop a prayer ministry in your congregation.

The best overall resource I can recommend is *Pray!* magazine, published by The Navigators. To access pertinent information about this resource and related ministries, go to www.praymag.com.

In addition to this foundational Web site, you may want to explore the following sites:

- www.prayerleader.com
- www.prayingpastor.com
- www.praykids.com
- www.nationalprayer.org
- www.globaldayofprayer.com

I also want you to know about The Upper Room Living Prayer Center in Nashville, Tennessee. This center receives thousands of prayer requests every month. The Prayer Center can train your congregation in the ministry of intercessory prayer and make your church a remote intercession center. For information about this ministry, go to www.upperroom.org/prayer_center.

The following books can help you develop a prayer ministry in your church.

Graf, Jonathan, and Lani C. Hinkle, eds. *My House Shall Be a House of Prayer*. Colorado Springs: NavPress Publishing Group, 2004.

Kamstra, Doug. *The Praying Church Idea Book: Practical Ways Your Church Can Pray*. Grand Rapids, MI: CRC Publications, 2001.

Teykl, Terry. *The Presence Based Church*. The Woodlands, TX: Prayer Point Press, 2003.

Vander Griend, Alvin J., and Edith Bajema. *The Praying Church Sourcebook*, 2nd edition. Grand Rapids, MI: CRC Publications, 1997.

Finally, I want to recommend a multimedia course on prayer that you will find helpful in launching a prayer ministry: *Learning to Pray Again* by Dr. Reg Johnson. You can order this resource directly from Dr. Johnson at Asbury Theological Seminary, 204 North Lexington Avenue, Wilmore, KY 40390.

ABOUT THE AUTHOR

STEVE HARPER is vice president and professor of spiritual formation at the Florida campus of Asbury Theological Seminary in Orlando. His education includes a PhD from Duke University, an MDiv from Asbury Theological Seminary, and a BA from McMurry University.

Dr. Harper is the author of numerous magazine articles and has authored and coauthored fifteen books, including *Devotional Life in the Wesleyan Tradition*, *Praying through the Lord's Prayer*, and *The Way to Heaven*. Over the years his ministry has focused on Christian spirituality, congregational transformation, and the application of Wesleyan theology to the life of the church.

Harper and his wife, Jeannie, have two grown children and two grandchildren.

OTHER TITLES OF INTEREST

To order any of these resources, call toll-free (800) 972-0433, or visit www.upperroom.org/bookstore.

Creating a Life with God: The Call of Ancient Prayer Practices
by Daniel Wolpert

Daniel Wolpert introduces you to twelve prayer practices that invite you to solitude and silence, to use your mind and imagination, to use your body and creativity, and to connect with nature and community.
ISBN 978-0-8358-9855-3 • Paperback • 192 pages

A Guide to Prayer for All Who Seek God
by Norman Shawshuck and Rueben P. Job

Like the other Guide to Prayer books (*A Guide to Prayer for All God's People* and *A Guide to Prayer for Ministers and Other Servants*), this devotional book follows the Christian year and the lectionary readings. Each week includes an invocation, a psalm, readings around a selected theme, daily scripture passages, reflection, prayers, a hymn, and a benediction.
ISBN 978-0-8358-1001-2 • Paperback • 430 pages

Traveling the Prayer Paths of Jesus
by John Indermark

John Indermark helps us walk the prayer paths of Jesus and gain insights into his prayer life. Readers see with fresh clarity that Jesus prayed at all times and in all places: for example, in the solitude of the desert and in the midst of crowds, on the mountaintop and in the garden. This six-week study provides prayer exercises that help individuals grow in their prayer lives.
ISBN 978-0-8358-9857-7 • Paperback • 208 pages

The Way of Prayer
by Jane E. Vennard

The Way of Prayer is a ten-week study designed to help people expand their understanding of the nature and practice of prayer. It offers many forms of prayer to explore and practice, both individually and as a group. People with different temperaments, spiritual types, and learning styles will each find expressions of prayer that draw them closer to God.

Participant's Book
ISBN 978-0-8358-9906-2 • Paperback • 142 pages

Leader's Guide *by Marjorie J. Thompson*
ISBN 978-0-8358-9907-9 • Paperback • 96 pages

Quiet Spaces: Prayer Interludes for Women
by Patricia Wilson

Wilson knows those days when the only quiet moment is that overlooked space, such as waiting for a dental appointment or while parked on a telephone hold. Her prayers in *Quiet Spaces* refresh the spirit in a short, beautiful way. Wilson's prayers give busy women the needed interlude of rest and time with God that their spirits so desire.
ISBN 978-0-8358-0969-6 • Paperback • 220 pages

When the Soul Listens

by Jan Johnson

Next Spiritual Formation
April 29 6:30